Dr. Hollis Lynch, Professor of History and Director of the Institute of African Studies at Columbia University, is the consultant for the Toward Freedom books. He brings to this program experience as a teacher, author, and editor of West African and Afro-American subjects. A native of Trinidad, Dr. Lynch's lifelong involvement in black history includes an active membership in the Association for the Study of Negro Life and History and the African Studies Association.

Toward Freedom Series

Their Eyes on the Stars

FOUR BLACK WRITERS

by Margaret Goff Clark

GARRARD PUBLISHING COMPANY
CHAMPAIGN, ILLINOIS

Library of Congress Cataloging in Publication Data

Clark, Margaret Goff.
    Their eyes on the stars: four Black writers.

    (Toward freedom series)
    SUMMARY: Traces the lives of four black writers who
wrote of the Negro experience in eighteenth- and nine-
teenth-century America.

    1. Hammon, Jupiter, 1711-ca. 1800—Juvenile litera-
ture. 2. Horton, George Moses, 1798?-ca. 1880—
Juvenile literature. 3. Brown, William Wells, 1815-
1884—Juvenile literature. 4. Chesnutt, Charles
Waddell, 1858-1932—Juvenile literature. I. Cary,
Louis F., 1915-   illus. II. Title. III. Series.

    PS153.N5C5   810′.9′896073 [B] [920] 73-3499
    ISBN 0-8116-4804-4

Acknowledgments

The author wishes to thank the following for their kindness
and help:

Robert H. Peer, Interlibrary Loans, Niagara Falls Public
Library

NIOGA Library System, Niagara County, New York

Buffalo and Erie County Public Library, Buffalo, New York

Laszlo L. Kovacs, Head of History, Biography, and Travel
Department, Cleveland Public Library, Cleveland, Ohio

Reference Department, The Library of Congress

University of North Carolina Library, Chapel Hill, North
Carolina

Mrs. N. H. Thigpen, Reference Librarian, Chesnutt Library,
Fayetteville State University, Fayetteville, North Carolina

Ann Allen Shockley, Head, Special Collections, and her
staff, at Fisk University Library, Nashville, Tennessee

Selections from the autograph album given to Charles W.
Chesnutt by his pupils are quoted from the album, which is
in the Charles W. Chesnutt collection at Fisk University

Contents

Black Voices

Black men and women came to America against their will, packed in slave ships. In the dark holds many of them died of hunger, overcrowding, or disease. The ones who lived were trapped in the prison of slavery from the moment they set foot on American soil.

Because their masters feared that an educated slave might become a troublemaker, few of these black Americans were taught to read and write.

It is not surprising then that these suffering people did not leave behind many books or poems. Rather, it is amazing that several eighteenth and nineteenth century blacks did produce literature and even had their works published. These writers gave voice to the longings of their people. Their pleas for freedom helped bring an end to slavery. After the Civil War their cry was for equality.

Like most literature of former days, the works of the early black writers are seldom read now. They wrote in the manner of their time, and their style seems out of date. Yet, the story of their struggle against discrimination, poverty, and lack of education is as inspiring today as it was when they lived.

In this book is the record of the lives of four of these black writers, beginning with Jupiter Hammon, the first American slave to see his own poetry in print. Born on Long Island in 1711, he had the advantage of a little more freedom and a little more education than most slaves. His writings were religious in theme, reaching toward the heaven where he firmly believed all men were free.

Almost ninety years later, George Moses Horton, a North Carolina slave, put his humor, his love of life and longing for freedom into verse.

William Wells Brown, the third of these early black writers, lived at about the same time as Horton. He began his long career of lecturing and writing for the cause of freedom after he escaped from his master and found refuge in the North.

The most fortunate and probably the best writer of the group was Charles Waddell Chesnutt, who was born in freedom just before the Civil War. His stories of the "color line," about black people of mixed blood, were well written and widely read.

The ground was—is—stony for blacks, but a few flowered in spite of difficulties. Why?

Some part of the answer may be found in the lives of these four writers.

Jupiter Hammon

AMERICA'S FIRST
BLACK POET IN PRINT

1. A Book of His Own

It was May 1733. The breeze from the Sound carried the scent of flowering fruit trees. Gulls wheeled overhead, and robins pecked the plowed ground for worms.

Jupiter Hammon was happy as he hurried home across the peninsula of Lloyd's Neck on the north shore of Long Island. In his hand he jingled the coins he had just received for working in a neighbor's garden. For months he had been saving money, coin by coin, to buy a Bible. Now at last he had enough.

Eager as he was to get home and claim his Bible, he sometimes slowed his pace to enjoy the beauty of the day. Jupiter was twenty-one and a slave. There were many joys in life he could never have; still it was his nature to appreciate every good thing that came along.

One thing that seemed especially good to him right now was that his master, Henry Lloyd, permitted him to earn money for himself by working for neighbors in his spare time.

When he reached home, he drew water from the well and washed. Then he went across the grass and beneath the locust trees to the Lloyd Manor House.

The house was built in 1711, the year Jupiter was born. Then in 1722 Mr. Lloyd rebuilt it. Now it was a large three-story mansion painted white. Splendid though it was, Jupiter felt at home in it. He knew every inch of the building. He had walked through the secret passageway that led underground to the harbor. He had stood at the dormer windows on the top floor, watching the boats move across the quiet, reed-edged waters of Lloyd's Harbor.

Now as Jupiter went toward the library to find his master, he remembered the day when Master Henry had showed him the ledger in which his birth was recorded. He had been only a boy at the time, just learning to read, so it had taken him a few minutes to study the list of names and birthdates of the Lloyd slaves. How pleased he had been when he found his own name. He had read aloud with pride: Jupiter Hammon, born October 17, 1711.

Jupiter Hammon was born a slave on this Long Island estate owned by Henry Lloyd.

"That's fine," Henry Lloyd had told him. "You're learning quickly. Soon you'll be able to read well enough to borrow some of my books."

Jupiter knew that few slaves were educated, but those who lived in Queen's Village, as the Lloyd estate was called, were fortunate. There was a school in the village to which Mr. Lloyd sent his slaves and his own children. Sometimes there was a shortage of schoolmasters. Then members of the Lloyd family taught the pupils at the school.

Jupiter learned to read well. Today as he

stepped into the library, the big, comfortable room had a welcoming look. He had been there many times before, and he knew what was between the covers of many of those books. Quite a few were about religion, for Henry Lloyd was a devout Christian.

"I have come to buy the Bible," said Jupiter. Months before he had asked Mr. Lloyd to order it for him, and he knew the book had arrived.

Carefully Jupiter counted out his money. "I have seven shillings and sixpence," he said.

"That's right," said his master, placing the book in his hands. "The Bible is yours."

Jupiter walked away in a daze, hugging the book to his chest. His hands caressed the leather cover as he tried to realize that this book actually belonged to him. He often had borrowed a Bible from his master, but now he had one of his own that he could read every night and morning. On Sunday, his one free day, he could spend hours memorizing his favorite verses.

2. "An Evening Thought"

Almost every Sunday morning Jupiter put on his best clothes and went to church. Sitting in one of the pews reserved for the slaves, he listened to the sermons and joyfully sang the hymns.

The words of the ministers had a deep effect on him. They promised a heaven where a slave could go and become a free man.

When the church service was over, Jupiter usually went home to study his own Bible. Soon the other slaves in Queen's Village discovered that Jupiter Hammon knew the Bible as well as any preacher. They began to ask him to explain the scriptures to them. He was glad to give little sermons to his friends, and gradually he became their "preacher."

Mr. Lloyd was pleased with his slave's intelligence and interest in religion. Since he, too, loved the Bible, he was glad to have his slave share this interest.

"My neighbors like to have you preach to their slaves," he told Jupiter.

Henry Lloyd recognized that Jupiter was a good man as well as a loyal slave. Because of this, he gave him many special privileges.

Late in his life Jupiter wrote: "I have great reason to be thankful that my lot has been so much better than most slaves have had."

New York State had many skilled slaves—harness makers, blacksmiths, farmers, and even silversmiths—but the profits from their work went to their masters.

Slaves, like Jupiter, who had some education were often permitted to preach to other slaves.

Jupiter was more fortunate than these other slaves. He took care of the trees in his master's orchard and was allowed to keep the earnings from the sale of the fruit.

He worked hard, and his master gave him free time for reading and writing.

Jupiter loved the hymns he sang in church, and he often made up words for the tunes he knew so well. Then he began to write poems on religious subjects. They were not based on hymns, but the

A N

Evening THOUGHT.

SALVATION BY *CHRIST*,

WITH

PENETENTIAL CRIES:

Compofed by Jupiter Hammon, a Negro belonging to Mr Lloyd, of Queen's-Village, on Long-Ifland, the 25th of December, 1760.

SALVATION comes by Jefus Chrift alone,
The only Son of God ;
Redemption now to every one,
That love his holy Word.
Dear Jefus we would fly to Thee,
And leave off every Sin,
Thy tender Mercy well agree ;
Salvation from our King.
Salvation comes now from the Lord,
Our victorious King ;
His holy Name be well ador'd,
Salvation furely bring.
Dear Jefus give thy Spirit now,
Thy Grace to every Nation,
That han't the Lord to whom we bow,
The Author of Salvation.
Dear Jefus unto Thee we cry,
Give us thy Preparation ;
Turn not away thy tender Eye;
We feek thy true Salvation.
Salvation comes from God we know,
The true and only One ;
It's well agreed and certain true,
He gave his only Son.
Lord hear our penetential Cry :
Salvation from above ;
It is the Lord that doth fupply,
With his Redeeming Love.
Dear Jefus by thy precious Blood,
The World Redemption have :
Salvation comes now from the Lord.
He being thy captive Slave.
Dear Jefus let the Nations cry,
And all the People fay,
Salvation comes from Chrift on high,
Hafte on Tribunal Day.
We cry as Sinners to the Lord,
Salvation to obtain ;
It is firmly fixt his holy Word,
Ye fhall not cry in vain.
Dear Jefus unto Thee we cry,
And make our Lamentation :
O let our Prayers afcend on high ;
We felt thy Salvation.

Lord turn our dark benighted Souls ;
Give us a true Motion,
And let the Hearts of all the World,
Make Chrift their Salvation.
Ten Thoufand Angels cry to Thee,
Yea louder than the Ocean.
Thou art the Lord, we plainly fee ;
Thou art the true Salvation.
Now is the Day, excepted Time ;
The Day of Salvation ;
Increafe your Faith, do not repine :
Awake ye every Nation.
Lord unto whom now fhall we go,
Or feek a fafe Abode ;
Thou haft the Word Salvation too
The only Son of God.
Ho ! every one that hunger hath,
Or pineth after me,
Salvation be thy leading Staff,
To fet the Sinner free.
Dear Jefus unto Thee we fly ;
Depart, depart from Sin,
Salvation doth at length fupply,
The Glory of our King.
Come ye Bleffed of the Lord,
Salvation gently given ;
O turn your Hearts, accept the Word,
Your Souls are fit for Heaven.
Dear Jefus we now turn to Thee,
Salvation to obtain ;
Our Hearts and Souls do meet again,
To magnify thy Name.
Come holy Spirit, Heavenly Dove,
The Object of our Care ;
Salvation doth increafe our Love ;
Our Hearts hath felt thy fear.
Now Glory be to God on High,
Salvation high and low ;
And thus the Soul on Chrift rely,
To Heaven furely go.
Come Bleffed Jefus, Heavenly Dove,
Accept Repentance here ;
Salvation give, with tender Love ;
Let us with Angels fhare.

F I N I S.

An original copy of Jupiter Hammon's Christmas poem, published as a broadside in 1761 beat of their rhythm was the same as that of the hymns.

Hammon celebrated Christmas Day, 1760, by writing a poem. He was then forty-nine years old. He called his Christmas poem "An Evening Thought. Salvation by Christ, with Penetential Cries."

The first eight lines are:

> *Salvation comes by Jesus Christ alone,*
> *The only Son of God;*
> *Redemption now to every one,*
> *That love his holy Word.*
> *Dear Jesus we would fly to Thee,*
> *And leave off every Sin,*
> *Thy tender Mercy well agree;*
> *Salvation from our King.*

The poem had many faults. Although every other line rhymed, the rhymes were not perfect, and in the eighty-eight lines of the poem, he used the word "Salvation" twenty-three times. In spite of its imperfections, the poem had a pleasing sound, especially when read aloud. Also, the earnestness of the writer was plain in every line.

Early in 1761 Henry Lloyd arranged to have the poem published in New York City as a broadside or broadsheet. This meant that Jupiter's poem was printed on one side of a large sheet of paper. Often 500 copies of such a sheet were printed at one time.

It was a proud moment for Jupiter when he held a copy of the broadside in his trembling hands and read:

AN EVENING THOUGHT.
SALVATION BY CHRIST,
WITH PENETENTIAL CRIES:
Composed by Jupiter Hammon, a Negro belonging to Mr. Lloyd of Queen's Village, on Long Island, the 25th of December, 1760.

The poem followed, printed in two columns.

Jupiter Hammon had good reason to be proud. He was the first black man to publish a poem in the American colonies.

3. War!

One day in March 1763, a woman slave stumbled down the steps of the Lloyd Manor House with tears streaming down her face.

Jupiter, who happened to be passing by, stopped to ask, "What's wrong?"

"It's master!" she sobbed. "What'll become of me now?"

Jupiter felt as if he had received a blow in the chest. "Master?" he asked.

The woman put her hands over her face. "He's gone! He breathed his last only a minute ago!" She ran away down the path leading to the slave quarters.

Jupiter did not move. Henry Lloyd was dead. Mr. Lloyd was seventy-seven and had been in poor health. The servants knew that he had brought his will up to date only a week ago. Still, his death was a shock. For all of Jupiter's life, Mr. Lloyd had been his master. It was like losing a father.

Jupiter went around the house to the back door to see if his help was needed. He was so wrapped in his sorrowful thoughts that he didn't realize that his face, too, was wet with tears.

Henry Lloyd's will stated: "My old Negroes are to be provided for." He wanted to be sure that the older slaves who had worked for him all their lives would be fed and clothed and housed even after they were unable to work. Some cruel men had been known to set their slaves free when they were too old or sick to be useful.

Henry had divided Lloyd's Neck among his four sons. To his son Joseph, he left Jupiter Hammon.

For several years after this, life for Jupiter was much the same as before. Then he began to hear people talking about the English king, George III, who was making the American colonies pay taxes on goods shipped to them.

It seemed as if Master Joseph and his brother Henry were constantly arguing these days. Henry said that the British were within their rights. Joseph declared that the colonies should be allowed to govern themselves and shouldn't have to pay taxes to a king on the other side of the Atlantic Ocean. People called Henry a Royalist or a Tory, while Joseph was labeled a Whig.

Jupiter then heard that because of the tax on tea, protestors had dumped the tea from a British ship in Boston harbor into the water. As punishment, the British Parliament passed a bill closing the port of Boston until the destroyed tea had been paid for.

There was more angry talk. More British soldiers arrived, and the Americans began to arm themselves.

Finally the British troops met the colonists in battle at Lexington, Massachusetts. War had begun.

After a year of fighting the colonists decided that they wanted more than an end to taxation by Britain. On July 4, 1776, their leaders signed a Declaration of

Independence which announced that the colonists wished to be free to govern themselves.

The war continued to spread throughout the thirteen colonies.

In August 1776, the British and the Hessian troops they had hired attacked Long Island and defeated the little American army at Brooklyn Heights. They set up camps at the western end of the island, and every day they came closer to Lloyd's Neck on the north shore. Whigs, like Joseph Lloyd, were in danger.

The fierce Battle of Long Island (below) forced the Lloyd family and their slaves to flee to Connecticut.

One day early in September Joseph told Jupiter and the other slaves that they must get ready to leave their homes. Joseph Lloyd and his family and slaves were going away from the island. They would cross Long Island Sound to Connecticut where the Americans were in control.

"Don't breathe a word of this to anyone," Lloyd warned. "If the enemy hear of my plans, they will try to stop me."

That night Jupiter made a bundle of his clothes and his Bible and walked down to the harbor.

On the shore men and women were hurrying back and forth in the dim light of hooded lanterns. Jupiter, who was still strong and healthy at sixty-four, helped to load the small boats that were waiting at the dock.

As the little fleet of boats pulled quietly away from shore, Jupiter wondered when he would see his home again. He hoped he would be back by spring in time to see the orchard in bloom.

For a time Joseph and his family and slaves stayed in Stamford, Connecticut. Then they moved to Hartford.

During the months and years that followed, Jupiter became acquainted with the people in the area. He began to preach to the slaves in Hartford. Some whites objected, saying he wasn't trained to be a preacher. But the slaves wanted him, and he continued to speak.

The Revolutionary War stirred up hopes of freedom in the slaves. If the whites were willing to fight so hard for liberty from England, couldn't they see that their own bondmen wanted liberty too?

Some white people understood the slaves' longing and tried to have laws passed toward freeing them. All of their attempts failed.

Many blacks were in despair, but others continued to hope that the end of the war would bring an end to slavery.

Jupiter shared these dreams, but had no wish to change his own life. He was more than sixty-five years old, and he was quite willing to serve Master Joseph for the rest of his days.

4. Poems and Sermons

At about this time Jupiter found a book that particularly pleased him. The book, called *Poems on Various Subjects: Religious and Moral*, was written by Phillis Wheatley.

Jupiter read the poems with special interest, for the young poet who had written this book was also black and a slave. She lived in Boston, Massachusetts.

The writings of Phillis Wheatley were a source of inspiration for Jupiter Hammon.

Hammon thought a great deal about Miss Wheatley. Her book had been published in England in 1773, and he understood that she had been there at the time. Her poetry told him that she was religious and that her ideas were much the same as his. How he wished he could meet her and talk about the joys and problems of writing!

His thoughts and longings led him to write a poem to Phillis Wheatley. With the help of Joseph

Lloyd and other friends, Jupiter's poem was published in Hartford as a broadside on August 4, 1778.

This is the way it began:

AN ADDRESS TO
MISS PHILLIS WHEATLY

O come you pious youth! adore
The wisdom of thy God,
In bringing thee from distant shore,
To learn His holy word.

Eccles. xii

Thou mightst been left behind
Amidst a dark abode;
God's tender mercy still combin'd,
Thou hast the holy word.

Psal. cxxxv 2,3

The poem had twenty-one verses, each with a reference to scripture. Verse number 17 urged Miss Wheatley to keep her thoughts on heaven:

While thousands muse with earthly toys;
And range about the street,
Dear Phillis, seek for heaven's joys,
Where we do hope to meet.

Matth. vi, 33

Critics think this poem is better written and shows more imagination than Jupiter's first published poem, "An Evening Thought." The poem to Miss Wheatley was well organized and had a theme—that God had brought her to the colonies where she could learn about Christ.

In 1779 Hammon published a prose piece, "An Essay on the Ten Virgins." No copy of it has been found, but a newspaper, *The Connecticut Courant,* advertised it for sale on December 14, 1779.

The war dragged on, and Master Joseph followed the war news anxiously. With every poor report on the fighting, he became more lost in gloom. If the British won, the property of American patriots would be taken from them, and their very lives would be in danger. A cloud of unhappiness settled over the Lloyd family and their slaves.

In the spring of 1780, the war news was especially bad. Charles Town, South Carolina, was under siege by the enemy, and in June word arrived that the city had surrendered. To Joseph Lloyd this meant that all hope was lost. Overwhelmed by despair, he took his own life.

Jupiter, now sixty-eight, was turned over to yet another master—John Lloyd, Jr., Joseph's nephew. Again there was little change in Hammon's life. He stayed in Hartford, and John proved to be a kindly master who, like Joseph, encouraged his talented slave.

Two years after the death of Joseph Lloyd, Jupiter published a prose sermon, "A Winter Piece."

On the first page of the little booklet is this statement:

> Written by Jupiter Hammon, A Negro Man belonging to Mr. John Lloyd, of Queen's Village, on Long Island, now in Hartford, Published by the Author with the Assistance of his Friends.

Jupiter began "A Winter Piece" with these words:

> As I have been desired to write something more than Poetry, I shall endeavor to write from these words, Matthew xi, 28. Come unto me all ye that labour and are heavy laden.

It was a rambling sermon with many references to scripture. Jupiter knew his Bible well.

In this same pamphlet Hammon included "A Poem for Children with Thoughts on Death."

One critic remarked that while this poem contained a warning to sinful children, it was quite playful in some lines. For instance:

> *Then shall ye hear the trumpet sound,*
> *The graves give up their dead,*
> *Those blessed saints shall quick awake,*
> *and leave their dusty beds.*
>
> *Then shall you hear the trumpet sound,*
> *and rend the native sky,*
> *Those bodies starting from the ground,*
> *In the twinkling of an eye.*

Jupiter signed one copy of this pamphlet for a minister he knew. On it he wrote in a strong, clear hand:

> For the Rev'd William Lockwood, from
> his firend* & humble Serv't, the Author.

In the spring of 1783, Jupiter with the "assistance of his friends," published another prose pamphlet, "An Evening's Improvement." Jupiter included in this booklet a poem, "A Dialogue Entitled the Kind Master and Dutiful Servant."

* Jupiter always had trouble with spelling.

AN

Evening's Improvement.

SHEWING,

The NECESSITY of beholding
the LAMB of GOD.

To which is added,

A DIALOGUE;

ENTITLED,

The KIND MASTER and
DUTIFUL SERVANT.

Written by JUPITER HAMMON, a Negro
Man belonging to Mr. *John Lloyd,* of Queen's
Village, on Long-Island, now in Hartford.

  HARTFORD:

Printed for the Author, by the Assistance of his Friends.

A rare copy of Jupiter's pamphlet, "An Evening's
Improvement," published in 1783

In this poem, which is very much like an English ballad, the master and servant take turns speaking to each other. The style of the poem leads critics to believe that Hammon had read English poetry.

At one point in the dialogue, Jupiter put in a word for his own preaching:

Believe me now, my Christian friends,
Believe your friend call'd Hammon:
You cannot to your God attend,
And serve the God of Mammon.

5. The Final Message

Jupiter Hammon laid out a pen, paper, and ink, and pulled a chair up to the kitchen table.

The Revolutionary War was over, and he was again living in Queen's Village.

He was almost seventy-five years old. Already he had lived longer than most people, and he was quite sure he didn't have much time left on earth. Before he died, there were several messages he wanted to leave for the benefit of his fellow slaves. There were things he had learned during his long life that he must pass on to them.

He wondered if he had the right to give advice to others, for he had had little schooling. Still, he reassured himself that many people, both black and white, had seemed to like the poems and sermons he had published in Hartford during the war.

Perhaps he could say things to other slaves that they would not accept from a white person. Also, though his words would be addressed to other black people, he had a message which he hoped many whites would take to heart.

He dipped his quill pen into the ink bottle and wrote: "An Address to the Negroes in the State of New York."

He began by telling of his pity for the unhappy conditions under which most of them lived. Then with sad patience he said:

> Now whether it is right, and lawful, in
> the sight of God, for them to make slaves
> of us or not, I am certain that while we
> are slaves, it is our duty to obey our
> masters . . .

He urged his fellow slaves to learn to read so they could study the Bible. Since they could expect nothing from the world, they should prepare for eternity where black and white people would be judged equally.

A N.

ADDRESS

TO THE

NEGROES

In the State of NEW-YORK,

By JUPITER HAMMON,

Servant of John Lloyd, jun, Esq; of the Manor of
Queen's Village, Long-Island.

" Of a. truth I perceive that God is no respecter of
" persons :
" But in every Nation, he that feareth him and
" worketh righteousness, is accepted with him,"—
Acts x. 34, 35.

NEW-YORK:

Printed by CARROLL and PATTERSON
No. 32, Maiden-Lane.

M,DCC,LXXXVII. 1787

The title page of Jupiter Hammon's *Address to the
Negroes in the State of New York*

In one of the strongest statements in the Address, he spoke about freedom:

> That liberty is a great thing we may know from our own feelings, and we may likewise judge so from the conduct of the white people in the late war. How much money has been spent, and how many lives have been lost to defend their liberty!

Jupiter remarked that he had hoped while the whites were fighting for liberty they would think of "the state of the poor blacks."

He urged that young blacks be set free, but said that "for my own part I do not wish to be free." He explained this by saying that "many of us who are grown up slaves, and have always had masters to take care of us, should hardly know how to take care of ourselves."

Hammon's "Address to the Negroes in the State of New York" was published in 1787 in New York City.

Slave owners read the Address to their slaves enthusiastically since it stressed obedience. But white Abolitionists and most blacks disliked many of Jupiter's ideas. They felt he was too humble, and they were especially disappointed that he said he did not wish to be free. However, some realized that at his age it was natural for him to fear being thrown unprepared into the world.

There were many people who thought that in spite of its mildness, Jupiter's Address was a valuable antislavery weapon. They believed it might help slave owners see how unfair it was to keep slaves. The Pennsylvania Society for the Abolition of Slavery immediately had the address reprinted in the city of Philadelphia.

Jupiter's deep sense of duty and loyalty to his master stayed with him all his life. Even when he had become a very old man, he continued to be a faithful worker.

One day in October 1790, Jupiter went to John Lloyd's house. His master had sent for him.

Mr. Lloyd handed him a small package. "I'd like you to take this to Oyster Bay," he said. He gave him further directions and told him to bring back a receipt.

Jupiter hitched a horse to the wagon and set off on his errand. Oyster Bay was a village a short distance to the west of Lloyd's Neck. Jupiter enjoyed the ride and the fine autumn day.

When he turned over John Lloyd's packet, he watched while the receipt was written. Then he carefully folded it and put it into his pocket.

As he traveled home, Jupiter thought, "Today is October 6. Why, in a few days I will be seventy-nine! Praise be to God! Few people live to be as old as that."

In 1806, sometime after Hammon's death, his Address was again reprinted, and that edition included a statement from three residents of Oyster Bay, Long Island, testifying that Jupiter was a good man and a good neighbor.

As time went on, Hammon's modest, quiet appeal to the white man's conscience began to take effect. He had said that young slaves should be given their liberty, and it is quite likely that this influenced his master. John Lloyd, in his will dated 1795, ordered that certain of his slaves be set free at the age of twenty-eight.

It is also believed that Jupiter's Address had something to do with the fact that in 1799 New York State began to pass laws toward gradually freeing the slaves in that state.

George Moses Horton

SLAVE POET OF CHAPEL HILL

1. A Slave's Day Off

The thin young slave toiled up the hill with his baskets of fruit and vegetables.

Ahead of him he saw the little village of Chapel Hill. The four large buildings at the very top of the hill must be the University of North Carolina. George Horton's heart beat faster, for he had built up great hopes for what he would find in this place.

When he reached the campus, he chose a comfortable spot under a huge oak tree. Here he set out the baskets of fruit and vegetables from his master's farm and sat down to wait for customers. Two other slaves were sitting not far away with their wares before them.

It was a fine autumn Sunday in 1816. As George watched, the chapel door opened, letting out a stream of young men, most of them dressed in neat blue suits. He thought they must be about the same age as he, but how different their lives were from his!

They came down the path toward George, and several stopped in front of him.

"Here's a new man—I think," said one of the students. "Have I seen you before?" he asked.

George answered solemnly, but with a twinkle in his eyes. "'By their fruits ye shall know them.'" He motioned to his basket of pears and apples.

The student stared at him, and then laughed. "Here's a black with an odd sense of humor. And a handsome fellow, to boot! What's your name?"

George made a deep bow. "George Moses Horton, sir, at your service."

The student turned to his friends. "Let's buy from George. I like his style."

Even after they had made their purchases—mainly fruit to eat between meals—the students stayed around George, talking with him. They seemed surprised to find a slave who had read several books and could quote from them.

When more students passed by, one boy called out, "Come here and listen to this fellow spout."

George was willing. He had asked his master's permission to come to Chapel Hill because he wanted to talk with the young men who were students there. He had heard they were interested in books and poetry, as he was.

The campus of the University of North Carolina at Chapel Hill, as it appeared in Horton's time

Encouraged by his audience, George talked and talked, using all the big words he had ever read. Sometimes he used them correctly, and sometimes he didn't. Whatever he said seemed to amuse the boys, and George liked having their friendly eyes fastened on him.

This was what he wanted—people who talked of books and who appreciated him. He almost forgot he was a slave.

There had been only one person to whom he had ever expressed himself like this, and that was his brother. When they were both children, George often talked with him about the beauty he saw in the sky and fields and of his desire for learning. But since they had grown up, the brothers saw little of each other.

On the Monday after he visited Chapel Hill, George found it harder than ever to go back to the fall plowing. All week while he worked for his master, James Horton, he thought about the hours he had spent in the college town.

It had been fun to make the boys laugh, but the more he thought about it, the less satisfied he was. He wanted more than their laughter. He wanted their respect. Some of the slaves who sold fruit at Chapel Hill would do anything to entertain the students. One even let the boys break boards over his head in return for a small fee.

George felt superior to these slaves. For one thing, he could read, and that was something few black men could do.

What a struggle he had had learning his letters! There had been no one to teach a young slave. He remembered how, when he was seven or eight, he had listened to the white schoolboys reading their lessons. Finally one of them gave him an old spelling book. Every Sunday after that he had gone alone into the woods where he sat all day studying the words.

Soon he mastered simple sentences, and then more difficult ones. After that he read everything he could find, but hymns and poetry were his favorites. Even part of a verse on a scrap of paper was a treasure to him, and he saved it.

George carried these bits of paper and pages from books with him wherever he went and studied them as he walked on errands for his master or while he ate his meals. At night he crouched over the light of a small fire reading, reading until his eyes burned from the smoke.

In his eagerness to learn and understand, he

George grew up as a slave in quarters similar to these. Here he taught himself to read and to make up poems.

often questioned the educated people he met about the meaning of difficult words and phrases.

George loved the sound of poetry and the ideas expressed in poems. To be a poet—ah—that would be wonderful! he thought.

Every now and then he tried putting his own ideas into verse. When he was alone, he spoke his poems out loud, and to him they sounded like the ones he read in books.

"I'm a poet!" he told himself with awe.

Lines came to him as he worked and when he lay down to sleep. His special talent for poetry became a shield against the hardships of his life as a slave.

2. Prove You're a Poet

The following Sunday George again walked the eight miles to Chapel Hill. This time when the students came to talk with him, he didn't try to make them laugh. Instead, he told them he was a poet, and to prove it, he recited one of his poems.

As he wrote later in his autobiography, ". . . all eyes were on me, and all ears were open."

But instead of praising him, the boys were silent until one of them cried out, "You didn't write that!"

"I don't know how to write," George admitted, "but I made the poem up in my mind."

"You read it someplace and memorized it!" another accused him.

George drew himself up proudly. "No, sir, that's not true. I have composed poems since I was a child. Why, I remember one I made up on a Sabbath morning when I was only a lad." He rushed on to quote the poem. The boys *must* believe him:

> *Rise up, my soul, and let us go*
> *Up to the gospel feast;*
> *Gird on the garment white as snow,*
> *To join and be a guest.*

> *Dost thou not hear the trumpet call*
> *For thee, my soul, for thee?*
> *Not only thee, my soul, but all,*
> *May rise and enter free.*

"All right, you have a good memory," said a tall young man. "But don't try to tell me you make up poetry. I never heard of any black poets."

"I have," put in another boy. "What about Phillis Wheatley up in Boston? She wrote a poem to George Washington, and she wrote lots of others besides."

"And Jupiter Hammon," said another. "He was a slave, and he wrote poetry before the revolution."

"All right," said the tall student. "But I won't believe George is a poet until he proves it."

George felt hurt and bewildered. If they wouldn't believe him when he quoted his own poems, how could he convince them he was a poet?

A well-dressed student who had stood in the rear of the group pushed his way to the front. "I know how George can prove he's a poet."

George turned his worried brown eyes to the young man's face.

"How?" demanded the tall student.

"By composing an acrostic," said the other with an air of triumph.

"Yes! That's the answer!" agreed the tall student.

The boys in the group seemed pleased, but George didn't understand until the boy explained.

"An acrostic is based on the letters of a word. Each line of your poem will begin with one of the letters in that word—in the correct order, of course."

George thought that this was an interesting idea. He loved a chance to exercise his quick mind. "What word?"

The student grinned. "Use my girl's name— Catherine. Now, you understand, your first line must begin with C and the second with A and so on."

George nodded. "You'll have to spell the name for me. Slowly, please, sir."

When he had memorized the spelling, he asked, "What would you like the poem to say?"

"Well, uh, make it a love poem I can send her." The young man reddened, and everyone laughed.

George worked all week over the acrostic. If he could go back to Chapel Hill next Sunday with a good poem about Catherine, the students would have to believe he was a poet.

Catherine's friend was waiting eagerly for his poem the following Sunday. He was ready with paper and goose-quill pen to write down the verse.

George closed his eyes to concentrate better and began to dictate the acrostic over which he had worked so hard.

When he had finished, the young student said warmly, "It's magnificent."

The tall young man who had loudly doubted that George was a poet came up to apologize.

"Chapel Hill has a black poet!" cried one boy. "Let's celebrate! I have some wine. Come on, George!"

George was willing, for he liked liquor and tended to drink too much of it. His master often gave it to the slaves.

Long after dark George followed the dirt road

back to Master Horton's plantation. His mind was clouded by the wine, but he remembered that he had orders for three more acrostics.

He was busy all the following week, composing the poems and memorizing them. When Sunday came, he dictated them without forgetting a word.

George Moses Horton's early acrostics have been lost, but one that he wrote later was saved. The girl's name was Julia Shepard, and the poem began:

Joy, like the morning, breaks from one divine—
Unveiling streams which cannot fail to shine.
Long have I strove to magnify her name
Imperial, floating on the breeze of fame.

George often used big words when a simpler word might have been more effective, but this was the style of much of the poetry of that day.

Almost every Sunday the young slave poet went to Chapel Hill. His master didn't mind as long as George took along some produce to sell to the students, faculty, and townspeople. After all, Sunday was a slave's day off.

Whenever George went to the campus, the students gathered around him and greeted him like an old friend. Although some laughed at the big words

A group of university students of pre-Civil War days. The young men at Chapel Hill helped George by giving him books and buying his poems.

he used, most of the boys tried to help him. George was grateful when they pointed out the errors in grammar and rhyme in his poems. Like any serious artist, he wanted to write as well as he could.

Soon his young friends began to bring him books that they thought he would like. He had never dared hope he would own so many—a dictionary, a grammar, a geography book, Milton's *Paradise Lost*, some of Shakespeare's works, a book of poems by Lord Byron, and many others. He found the geography especially useful. He might never see the places described, but he could use the names in his poems. In the dictionary he found more of the big words he loved.

One day a student named Augustus Alston suggested that George should be paid twenty-five cents for each poem, and the other students agreed. This was fairly good pay in those days, for often a college student's allowance was only one dollar a month.

George wrote in his autobiography many years later that ". . . some gentlemen, extremely generous, have given me from fifty to seventy-five cents, besides many decent and respectable suits of clothes."

The girls who received George's poems were pleased, so the students asked for more and more. Often George went home with orders for as many as twelve poems to compose during the week. He was making more money than he had ever had in his life.

He enjoyed having some change in the pockets of his suits, but most of all he was pleased that the boys valued his poems enough to pay for them. Each twenty-five-cent piece was proof that his work was worthwhile. In his autobiography he remarked:

> . . . my fame soon circulated like a stream throughout the college. . . . I have composed love pieces in verse for courtiers from all parts of the state, and acrostics on the names of many of the tip top belles of Virginia, South Carolina and Georgia.

George felt a growing pride in himself. He had been born a slave and had never had a day in school, but with almost no help he had learned enough to talk as an equal with college students. Indeed, he was a better poet than any student he met.

He was friendly with the other slaves, but after five or six years of visiting the university town, he no longer had much in common with them. Although he spent only one day a week at Chapel Hill and six days on the plantation, his thoughts were always on his poetry and the students for whom he wrote.

3. New Friends

One Sunday George Horton was alone at his usual spot under the oak tree when a pleasant-looking man stopped to look at his fruit. George recognized him at once as Joseph Caldwell, the president of the university. He was flustered at having such an important customer, but he didn't lose his usual good manners.

"Good morning, President Caldwell," he said. "Can I help you?" He picked out the reddest apple he could find and offered it to him. "Would you care to try that, sir?"

"Thank you, George." President Caldwell bit into the fruit and chewed thoughtfully. "Excellent. I'd like a dozen of those apples. I guess you're surprised that I know your name," he continued. "But I've heard a lot about you and your remarkable poems. Are you familiar with the poetry of Lord Byron?"

George soon forgot his embarrassment, and the two men talked together for some time. When George asked about some passages in Shakespeare and Homer that had been puzzling him, the president seemed glad to explain.

Before he left, President Caldwell said, "You're welcome here, George. If you ever have any problems, come to see me about them. You know where I live?"

He motioned toward an ordinary-looking house that stood near the college buildings.

"Yes, thank you, I do," George replied. "Perhaps there are some odd jobs I could do around the house?"

"Perhaps there are," agreed Mr. Caldwell. "I'll keep you in mind."

After that, the president made a habit of stopping to talk to George. Often he brought along a book for him to read. When he discovered that George couldn't write, he began to help him to learn.

George was grateful for Joseph Caldwell's interest in him. As a result of it, even the students who thought George was a joke treated him with more respect. And as the months and years passed, George carried himself with growing dignity. George Moses Horton became an accepted part of the scene at Chapel Hill.

Sometimes when his fruit was sold, he knocked at the president's door to see if he had some work to be done. George did this only to show his gratitude, but Mr. Caldwell usually insisted on paying him.

As kind as President Caldwell was, George was not prepared for the friendliness of a new faculty member and his wife who came to Chapel Hill in the autumn of 1826.

George was thirty and had been visiting the

university town for ten years when Mr. and Mrs. Nicholas Hentz arrived. Mr. Hentz was a teacher of languages, and his wife Caroline was a poet.

Only a few weeks after their arrival, the Hentzes invited George to Sunday afternoon tea. A few friends were coming in to talk about books and poetry, they said. Perhaps George would enjoy the conversation.

George was amazed. White people in North Carolina didn't ask slaves to call at their homes unless they had some work to be done.

At first he thought he wouldn't go. How should he behave? What could he say? Surely the other guests would snub him. Finally curiosity won. George decided to go.

He went to the back door of the Hentz home, but Caroline Lee Hentz greeted him warmly and led him into the parlor where several teachers were talking and drinking tea. They seemed to expect him, and though their greeting was brief, they didn't leave, as he had feared they might.

Mrs. Hentz drew him to one side. "I have read some of your poems," she said, "and I admire your work. Is it true that you're a slave?"

"Yes," said George in his formal way. "I've been in bondage all my life." He remained on his feet, though she had motioned him to a chair.

Caroline Lee Hentz (top) and her husband, Nicholas, encouraged George in his desire to write poetry.

The attractive young woman looked at him with pity in her eyes. "Your poems show a great love of life. I don't see how you can write in slavery."

George smiled. "The birds sing for slaves too, and the flowers share their fragrance with us."

She laughed. "Spoken like a true poet!"

Encouraged by her interest, George found himself telling her about his family—his four sisters and his brother, all younger than he—and how his mother had done her best to raise them alone. He had scarcely known his father, for, as was often the case with slaves, his father had become separated from his family.

"I've known trouble," George told Mrs. Hentz, "but it always inspired me to write poetry. When things are at their worst, that's when I write the best."

As he walked home late that afternoon, George could think of nothing but his kind and brilliant new friend. Not even the autumn red of the maples and the russet of the oaks could turn his mind away from his glorious hours in the Hentz parlor.

How sympathetic she had been when he had told her he was a slave!

He thought of the dainty sandwiches she had served and the tea that was like the nectar of the gods. That was the world where he belonged—the world of quiet voices and intelligent conversation.

He groaned aloud when he thought of the shack where he lived and the week of work ahead. Field work had always been drudgery to him, and now he liked it less. Slavery had become unbearable.

If only he were free, he could spend all of his time at Chapel Hill, writing and selling poetry and talking with interesting people like Mrs. Hentz.

He must find a way to get his freedom!

4. Poems for Freedom

Almost every Sunday George visited Mrs. Hentz. Since she was a good poet, she was able to make suggestions for improving his poetry. And she, like President Caldwell, gave him lessons in writing.

The students, telling George the gossip of the university, remarked that there were many faculty homes where the Hentzes were not invited to go.

"They're too free in their thinking for most people around here," one boy told George. "Mr. Hentz is from France, and you know how broad-minded the French are!"

"And Mrs. Hentz," added another student. "She's from New England, and she's a freethinker like her husband. They're an interesting pair. I hear he's a scientist, and he runs all over the countryside collecting spiders. He's making a study of them." He looked curiously at George. "You go to their house. Who else goes? Do you see any of the faculty there?"

"Of course," said George haughtily. "The most intelligent people for miles around meet at the Hentzes. Mr. and Mrs. Hentz don't need to worry about a few people who don't know enough to appreciate them."

In spite of his confident answer, he worried that his visits to their home might be one of the reasons the Hentzes were unpopular with some of the faculty. But when he mentioned this to Caroline Hentz, she told him that she would see whomever she pleased in her home, and it was her pleasure to see him.

The people who gathered in the Hentz parlor on Sunday afternoons to talk of science with Nicholas and literature with Caroline gradually accepted George's presence. He was a slim, good-looking man with medium brown skin, and they found his manner charming. They enjoyed his witty conversation and often laughed at his humorous remarks, but they listened when he was serious too.

Although he sometimes put on lordly airs around the other slaves, he was more natural when he visited the Hentzes. Caroline wrote several years later that George Moses Horton was "unpretending" and that he had the "mild gravity of a Grecian philosopher."

In the summer of 1827, Caroline's oldest child,

a little boy who was almost two, fell from a chair. He broke a bone in his neck and died instantly.

George could think of nothing but his friend's grief, and he did the only thing he could to help her. He composed a poem about the death of the child. The next time he saw Mrs. Hentz, he dictated it to her, for he still couldn't write.

The tears ran down Caroline's cheeks as she wrote the words, but she was grateful for his concern, and gave him, as he later wrote, "much credit and a handsome reward."

With every visit to Chapel Hill and the Hentzes, George longed more intensely for his freedom. As he searched his mind for ways to become free, he wondered if his poetry could possibly help him.

He began to make up poems about slavery and recited some of them to Caroline Lee Hentz. One of the verses especially moved her:

> *Alas! and am I born for this,*
> *To wear this slavish chain?*
> *Deprived of all creature bliss,*
> *Condemned to toil and pain.*

Mrs. Hentz asked his permission to send the poem to a newspaper.

A few Sundays later when George went to the Hentz home, Caroline Hentz brought out a copy of the *Lancaster Gazette*, published in Lancaster, Pennsylvania. In it were two poems by George Moses Horton and a short article about him.

The guests at the Hentz house praised him, and Mrs. Hentz gave him the newspaper to keep.

On the way home he stopped beside the road to read again the two poems and the article. There was his name in clear print. Hundreds—maybe thousands—of people would read his words and the article about him. It was exciting to realize that he was becoming known by people he had never seen. Perhaps in some way this might lead to his freedom.

Sometime later the *Register*, a newspaper in Raleigh, North Carolina, carried one of George's poems and an article about his life. Other newspapers in the area copied them.

One man, a visitor to Chapel Hill, identified only as a "philanthropic gentleman," read George's poems and decided that the poet should be free. He wrote to James Horton asking if he would sell his poetic slave. James replied that he might sell George at the end of the farming season.

The interested "gentleman" gave this information to some of George's friends, who were delighted with the idea of setting their poet free. At once they started trying to raise funds. Among these friends were students, former students, and Chapel Hill faculty members. Some money even came from people George didn't know—people in the North and the South who had read his poems and thought he should be free. The fund grew faster than George's friends had dared hope.

It looked as if George's dreams were coming true at last, and he began to make plans for his life as a free man. He had heard about Liberia, an African colony for free blacks, and he thought he might like to go there to live.

But James Horton wanted a large sum for his famous slave, and George's friends couldn't collect enough money to pay for his freedom.

George's spirits sank low, but his friends didn't give up. They took up another collection for the poet and finally had enough to pay for publishing a book of his poems.

"You'll sail to Liberia on your own words," they told him.

In 1829 George Moses Horton's book, *The Hope of Liberty*, was published. It contained poems on the trials of slavery, but also touched on love, religion, death, and nature.

One of the poems in the book, "On the Poetic

The life of a slave on a tobacco plantation had become more and more painful for the black poet.

Muse," contained some of George's own thoughts about writing poetry:

My towering thoughts with pinions rise,
Upon the gales of song,
Which waft me through the mental skies,
With music on my tongue.

And when the vain tumultuous crowd
Shakes comfort from my mind,
My muse ascends above the crowd
And leaves the noise behind.

It was a thin little book containing only twenty-two pages. Still George took great satisfaction in it, for newspapers were read and thrown away, but books were kept for years and handed down from father to son. In a way a poet lived forever, thought George. And of course this book was special, for it was going to buy his freedom.

But *The Hope of Liberty* didn't sell enough copies to buy George's freedom. George feared that he would never be free.

Caroline Hentz tried to console him. "George, sometimes I think you're better off as a slave," she said. "Your master is kind to you, and he'll always see to it that you have a place to live and food to eat."

George was surprised to hear her say this, for she had always seemed to understand his every emotion. Perhaps, he reasoned, someone who had always been free couldn't realize that it was better to starve in freedom than feast in slavery. And slaves rarely feasted!

George's book failed to set him free, but it made him even more of a star in Chapel Hill. Few men, black or white, had a book of poetry in print.

Soon several things happened that made achieving freedom even more unlikely. In 1830 a pamphlet urging blacks to revolt and murder whites was distributed in the South. When this booklet was discovered in North Carolina, a frightened state legislature passed a law making it illegal to teach black people how to read and write.

In 1831 a Virginia slave named Nat Turner led a revolt in which many white people were killed. As a result more laws were passed in the southern states cutting down still further the rights of the blacks. One law required that when a slave was freed, he must leave the state within ninety days, never to return.

James Horton may have thought this was no time to set free a slave who could read and could even compose poetry. Or perhaps he was afraid George wouldn't be able to make a living if he were sent out of the state. At any rate, he refused to sell George,

Joseph Caldwell, president of the University of North Carolina, became George's friend and benefactor.

though he did allow him more freedom to come and go as he wished.

Some people laughingly said that George Moses Horton owned James Horton and practically owned President Caldwell of Chapel Hill. But George was thirty-four years old and still a slave. He wanted more than a little freedom.

His gloom was even deeper because in 1831 Caroline and Nicholas Hentz and their children moved from Chapel Hill to Kentucky. Their five years of friendship had changed George's life.

In his autobiography George wrote that he would never forget Caroline Hentz's aid as long as he lived.

Out of his great feeling of loss, George wrote a poem in praise of his friend. He was able to put it onto paper himself, for now at last he could write.

The poem began:

Deep on thy pillar, thou immortal dame,
Trace the inscription of eternal fame;
For bards unborn must yet thy works adore,
And bid thee live when others are no more.

Two years after she moved, Caroline Lee Hentz published *Lovell's Folly*, the first of her many novels. In this book she wrote admiringly of George Moses Horton.

5. Hard Times

George had not won his freedom, but he still had hopes of spending more time at Chapel Hill. With this hope in mind, he went to James Horton.

"Master," he said, "I'd like to hire out my time. I would pay you twenty-five cents a day if you'd let me off work in the fields."

James Horton thought this over. It was now

against the law to let a slave pay his master for the privilege of working for someone else, but it was often done, just the same. Now that all of George's thoughts were on poetry and Chapel Hill, he wasn't much help on the farm, anyway. James agreed to George's plan.

For a few years, all went well. George sold several poems a day and found it easy to put away a quarter for his master. He sometimes did odd jobs for President Caldwell and other faculty members to make a little extra money. With this occasional work and his poetry writing, he earned enough to keep a roof over his head and to pay for food and clothing.

But one morning early in 1835, when George Horton arrived on the campus, he noticed that everyone seemed troubled. People were gathered in quiet groups under the winter trees or in doorways.

"What's wrong?" George asked a student. "Why does everyone look like doomsday?"

The student stopped. "Haven't you heard, George? President Caldwell died." The young man shifted his books. "Things will never be the same around here without him."

At first George felt dazed. He mumbled a thank you to the student, and when the boy had gone on, George still remained in the path, staring at the brown oak leaves that lay on the ground at his feet.

He repeated to himself, "Things will never be the same."

They never would be the same for him, he knew. He felt a heaviness in his chest as he thought of the kindly man who had so often stopped to chat with him. President Caldwell had let everyone in Chapel Hill know that he was George Horton's friend.

Spring came to Chapel Hill that year as usual, but George's life was wintry.

One April afternoon when the flowering dogwood trees shone like clouds among the dark oaks and pines, George followed a path toward one of the buildings where the students had rooms. The few boys he saw hurried by with only a quick greeting. Their attitude had changed since President Caldwell's death.

The new president, David Swain, was kind enough, and the students seemed to like him, but George didn't feel close to him as he had to President Caldwell.

The students weren't full of fun anymore either, thought George. They always had their minds on their studies, and they weren't buying poems anymore.

George took a job as a servant to earn money for food, room rent, and his master's twenty-five cents a day. Still, he couldn't make ends meet. When George was unhappy, he drank more, and liquor was expensive.

He had taken a drink to give him courage before he started out this afternoon, and his steps weren't quite steady as he climbed the stairs to the residence hall. He stopped at the first open door and coughed slightly to attract the attention of the student who was bent over a book at his desk.

"I have a poem here for you to read, sir," said George.

The student looked up. "Good afternoon, George. Sorry. I'm awfully busy. Some other time."

George didn't move. "It won't take a minute."

The student shook his head.

"I'll read it to you." Without waiting for an answer, George began to read his poem aloud. All of its several verses told how much he needed money.

The student sighed and got slowly to his feet. He held out a coin. "Here you are, George."

George looked at the money. He was disappointed to see that it was only ten cents, but he said politely, "Thank you, sir," and shuffled down the hall.

Every door he passed was closed. That was strange. He was sure several had been open before.

The students were avoiding him—that was it. The very same boys who had come around begging for his poems and paying him handsomely for them were hiding from him now.

He went sadly back to his room and had another drink from his bottle.

Although things were going badly for George Horton in Chapel Hill, he was now becoming famous in the North. In 1837, when he was forty years old, his book of poetry, *The Hope of Liberty*, was reprinted in Philadelphia under the title *Poems by a Slave*. The following year these poems were published in the same book with works by Phillis Wheatley, the well-known black poet.

His poems also were printed by those newspapers in the North that were interested in bringing an end to slavery.

George, who probably didn't know of his fame, sometimes thought that nothing in his life was working out right. He was married unhappily to a woman who was the slave of Franklin Snipes, a neighbor of James Horton. He had to admit to himself that he didn't help her very much, but on the other hand, he might as well not have a wife for all the attention she paid him. He saw little of her or his two children, who were named Snipes after their mother's master.

George's unfortunate marriage made him bitter about women. When a student asked for a love poem, George made it sweet and romantic, but when he wrote a poem just for his own pleasure, he generally poked fun at marriage. One such poem was called "Pleasures of a Bachelor's Life," and in it he advised bachelors to remain unmarried . . .

Without a surly wife to scold
Or children to disturb your mind,
To pillage o'er your chest for gold
And spend for trifles what they find.

6. Farewell to Chapel Hill

When George was forty-six years old, his master, James Horton, died. Hall Horton, a son of James, became George's new master.

Immediately Hall announced that George must now pay fifty cents a day for his freedom from farm work.

George was frantic. That was twice what he had been paying! How could he manage? He *had* to find a way. He thought, "If I cut down on drinking, I can save some money. And I'll put out another book."

He gathered poems for a book, but he couldn't find anyone who wanted to print it.

This time the students at Chapel Hill came to his aid. Even though they avoided him when he came begging for money, they admired his jaunty courage and his poetry. They raised enough to publish a collection of his poems which was called *The Poetical Works of George M. Horton, the Colored Bard of North Carolina.* George wrote a short autobiography which was included in the book.

Some of the poems in *The Poetical Works* were humorous. One of them showed that he could even laugh at his shortage of money:

> **The Woodman and the Money Hunter**
> *The woods afford us much supply,*
> *The opossum, coon, and coney;**
> *They all are tame and venture nigh,*
> *Regardless of the public eye,*
> *I know but one among them shy,*
> *There's nothing shy but money.*

The little book sold for only fifty cents, but not enough copies were purchased to help the poet very much.

Still, George refused to leave the life and people he loved to return to farm work. He stayed at Chapel Hill, carrying wood for fires in the winter and weeding gardens in the summer. He peeled potatoes and washed dishes and repaired fences.

He was drinking very little. He couldn't afford liquor, and he realized now that it kept him from

* rabbit

doing his best writing. In a poem that was included in his *Poetical Works*, he looked squarely at his problem:

The Tippler to His Bottle

Often have I thy stream admired;
Thou nothing has availed me ever;
Vain have I thought myself inspired,
Say, have I else but pain acquired?
Not ever, no never!

Gradually the sale of his poems to students increased. Again the boys flocked around him. Perhaps this happened because he was drinking less or perhaps because a new group of boys had come to Chapel Hill.

In 1849 the students of the university asked him to give the Independence Day address.

On the morning of that Fourth of July, George Horton looked quite distinguished as he set out for Gerrard Hall. He had carefully trimmed the frayed edges of the well-made suit given him by one of the students. Now fifty-two, he was still straight, slim, and good looking.

George was aware that he was probably the first slave to be asked to give an address at the university, and he was nervously eager to do well.

A group of students met him at the hall. They

put him at the head of a procession and directed him to a seat on the platform.

George's knees shook as he rose to speak, but he reminded himself that these were his friends. There was no need to feel afraid.

His talk lasted only five minutes, but the boys seemed to like it. He thought the applause would never end. Afterward some of the boys walked down the street with him.

"You were a great success, George," one of them told him. "They clapped fifteen minutes by my watch."

For a few years George continued to sell many poems. The college was growing, and the students were from well-to-do families.

In spite of his success, freedom was constantly on George's mind.

It wasn't fair! He was in his fifties, a poet whose books had been published. Articles about him had appeared in the newspapers. And still he was a slave.

He went to his master, Hall Horton, to tell him of his great desire for freedom.

Surprisingly Hall agreed to sell him for $250 if George could find a buyer.

George went up the hill again, going over in his mind a list of men he knew who might have that much money. His hope was that someone might buy him and then give him his freedom. But no one wanted to spend so much to set a black poet free.

"You're doing all right," they told him. "You're just as good as free right now. And if times get hard, you can always go back to your master."

Again George had failed to get his freedom. He stayed at Chapel Hill for ten more years.

Although he had many friends among the students, faculty, and townspeople, he was no longer well liked by his fellow slaves. He had always felt superior to the other slaves, but now he passed them without speaking. It seemed that his repeated failure to obtain his freedom had made him bitter, and he took out his anger on those who were worse off than he was.

George's years at Chapel Hill came to an end with the firing on Fort Sumter in April 1861. The students left the campus in great numbers, most of them to join the Confederate forces.

With the boys gone, George could no longer make a living in the university town. He was past sixty when he went back down the hill and walked the eight miles to Hall Horton's plantation.

Hall took him in, but he was disgusted with his old slave. George wasn't strong enough for heavy field work, and he had had no training for anything else. The other slaves, long scorned by him, didn't welcome him. George's dreams of a better life seemed farther away than ever.

The war had driven George from Chapel Hill, but the actual fighting never came near the county where he lived. While the armies of the North and the South clashed at Bull Run, Antietam, Gettysburg, and Vicksburg, George was absorbed in his own struggle.

He had been the Prince of Poetry on Chapel Hill, but on the farm he was a misfit. If he hoed corn or picked tobacco, he always fell behind the others, and his master would shout for him to work faster.

"You're not worth your keep!" Hall would declare. "I ought to put you out to starve."

On Sundays George often trudged back to Chapel Hill to see if any of the boys had returned, but the university remained deserted. The four years of war seemed endless to George.

At last, in April 1865, word reached the plantation that the war was over. Lee had surrendered to Grant at Appomattox Courthouse. The North had won, and the slaves were free. The Yankee soldiers were coming to Chapel Hill to serve as a village guard.

George could scarcely believe this wonderful news. He gathered his poems and extra clothes into a bundle and set out on foot. Other blacks were on the road too.

At the end of the war, George joined the other freed slaves streaming toward Union Army positions.

"We're free!" they all shouted to one another.

George found it hard to realize that after sixty-eight years as a slave, he was free. He could go to Chapel Hill without paying his master fifty cents a day.

Of course his master would no longer give him room and board, but George wasn't afraid. He was sure he could always make a living with his poetry.

7. Poet Horton

As George neared Chapel Hill, he saw a soldier in a blue uniform talking to a group of former slaves.

"Go back to your old masters," the Union soldier urged. "Stay with your regular jobs for a while. We can't take care of all of you."

Most of the blacks pushed on, shaking their heads. They wouldn't return to slavery just to be sure of a bed and something to eat. George, too, hurried on.

Union soldiers were everywhere in their blue uniforms. To George they looked very much like the Chapel Hill students, and he was sure he would find a friend among them.

He talked to the soldiers and showed them his poems. Some took the time to listen to the scholarly-looking, gray-haired black man and to glance at his poems. Others ignored him. But one young soldier sat down with him and went through the sheets of poetry with interest.

"I'm Captain Will Banks," he said, looking up at George with friendly interest. "What is your name?"

"George Moses Horton, poet," replied George.

"You were a slave?"

"All my life, and I'm well over sixty."

"I've been fighting in this war for a long time," said Captain Banks, "and sometimes I've wondered if our cause was worth all the suffering I saw." His gaze dropped to the poems he still held. "Now when I read these and see you, I know it was all worthwhile."

George knew he had found his friend. He stayed with Captain Banks for the short time that the Ninth Michigan Cavalry Volunteers remained in Chapel Hill.

When Captain Banks left, so did George. It was spring, and the dogwood and redbud trees were in bloom. As the soldiers marched along, George sold them poems.

Captain Banks wanted him to write some more poems about the war and the peace. Then he planned to have a book of Horton's poems printed to prove that the blacks had talent that rarely had a chance to develop under slavery.

As soon as Banks was mustered out of the army, he and George went to Raleigh, North Carolina, where he arranged for Horton's book, *Naked Genius*, to be printed. This book of 132 poems was published in 1865.

Like *Hope of Liberty*, it included poems on many themes.

Many of the poems in *Naked Genius* revealed Horton's sense of humor. His wit was often aimed at women:

> *Woman, thou bloom of every danger,*
> *From whose charms my sorrows rise,*
> *To thee I'd live and die a stranger;*
> *He who shuns thee must be wise.*

Captain Banks returned to his home in Michigan, and George went to Philadelphia where many former slaves had gone to live. There, on August 31, 1866, the Banneker Institute, a literary club made up of thirty educated black men, gave a reception in George's honor. George amused the people at the gathering by his remark that his master had reckoned his age by looking into his mouth and judged the state of his health by whipping him. He still loved to make people laugh, even if he sometimes had to stretch the truth to make them do it.

Over the years several George Moses Hortons shared one thin body. One was the clown who followed the spotlight. Another was weak and drank to escape reality. But there was a deeper George who struggled to put into words his unique and often humorous view of life, as well as his hunger for freedom.

Although he seemed to speak only for himself, his poetry gave voice to the longings of thousands of slaves. All over the country readers of Horton's poems were awakened to the hidden talents of black people.

George was always proud of being a poet. In 1883 Collier Cobb, a Chapel Hill professor, saw him in Philadelphia and called him "Poet."

George replied, "That pleases me greatly, Professor Cobb. You are using my proper title."

These are his last recorded words. We believe he died later that year at the age of eighty-six.

ANTI-SLAV
MEETIN

BUFFALO, N
WM. WELLS BROWN

William Wells Brown

FREEDOM'S CHAMPION

1. The Right to Liberty

William knew the boys were waiting for him. They stood close to a building, making snowballs and packing them hard. William was fifteen and almost as large as the white boys, but there were several of them.

He plodded on, clutching the form of type he was carrying to the newspaper office where he worked. His master, Dr. John Young, often sent him out to work for other people, for he was intelligent and could earn good wages. Since he was a slave, his salary, of course, was paid to Dr. Young.

William liked his present job as helper and errand boy to the editor Elijah Lovejoy. The office of the *St. Louis Times* was an interesting place, and there, at last, he was learning to read and write.

On this winter day in 1830, he had gone on an errand to another newspaper. He was in a hurry to get back to the office with the page of type for Mr. Lovejoy, and he hoped the boys wouldn't try to stop him.

Although the boys stared at the sky or the ground as he passed, William knew they were only pretending to ignore him. He wanted to run, but his burden weighed him down. The metal frame that held the page of type together was heavy, and the type metal itself was even heavier.

He was ten feet beyond the boys when the first snowball thudded against his back. Seconds later a rock struck him on the head, and he fell to his knees. The boys closed in on him.

There was only one thing to do. William laid the form of type on the ground and stood up to fight off his attackers. When at last he was able to break away, he fled up the street.

Looking back from a safe distance, he saw that the boys had picked up the type form. He hated to return to the office without the type, but there was no way to get it back. He felt especially sorry because Mr. Lovejoy was the kindest man for whom he had worked. Although he was white, he seemed to understand the feelings of a slave, and he had even written articles for his newspaper declaring that all slaves should be set free. In 1830 this was a dangerous thing to say in a slaveholding state like Missouri.

At the office of the *St. Louis Times*, William told the editor what had happened. At once Mr. Lovejoy ran outside and disappeared down the snowy street.

When he returned, he had the form of type. He had talked with a man named McKinney, the father of one of the boys who had attacked William. Mr. McKinney had said that William had hurt his son, and he planned to get even.

Several days later as William was walking along Main Street, he felt a hand on his shoulder and the next thing he knew a heavy cane came down on his head again and again.

He managed to drag himself, bleeding, to the office. Mr. Lovejoy helped him into a carriage and had him taken back to his master, Dr. Young. It was five weeks before he was again strong enough to work. Then, to his disappointment, he learned that his place at the newspaper office had been filled.

Dr. Young quickly found his slave another job, this time as a steward on the *Enterprise,* a steamboat that traveled up and down the Mississippi River.

William liked the job in many ways, but as he served the white men on the boat and listened to their talk of places they had been, he wished that he, too, were free to come and go. He wished that he could keep the money he earned as they did.

William served as a steward in the dining room of a Mississippi river steamboat like this one.

On the Fourth of July the *Enterprise* was tied up at a St. Louis wharf. William went ashore to watch the celebration, and there he heard a speech that changed his life.

"Our Declaration of Independence says all men are created equal!" the speaker, a Missouri senator, declared.

Equal? thought William. All men? That would include him!

"And they are endowed by their Creator with certain unalienable rights," continued the senator. "Among these are life, liberty, and the pursuit of happiness!"

One word stood out among all the others—liberty! If liberty was the right of every man according to the Declaration of Independence, then slavery was wrong.

At that moment William vowed to himself, "I'm going to be free!"

2. Escape

Escape! It was always on William's mind. When the *Enterprise* docked at ports near the free states of the north, he had several good chances to run away. But he waited, for he didn't want to go while his mother, sister, and brothers were still slaves.

Then the captain of the *Enterprise* left the ship, and William was returned to his master, Dr. Young. Now he could not escape, but at least he was given interesting work.

Dr. Young made him his medical assistant with the other slaves as his patients. He later wrote about one of his experiences as a part-time doctor:

> Sometimes I committed sad mistakes, through my ignorance of the profession. On one occasion, being ordered by the doctor to extract a slave's tooth, I laid the patient flat on his back on the floor,

got astraddle of his breast, put the rusty
turn-keys on the wrong tooth, and pulled
with all my strength. The result was, I
took out a sound grinder . . .

His career in medicine was short, for Dr. Young
needed money and sold William to a man who later
sold him again.

William's third master was Enoch Price, owner
of the steamboat *Chester*, which carried passengers and
cargo from New Orleans to Cincinnati, Ohio. Price took
William on board as a steward.

On the night of December 31, 1833, William
stood on the deck of the *Chester*. About three years
had passed since the Fourth of July when he had made
up his mind to escape. He gazed across the dark water
at the shore. Out there was Ohio, a free state. Tomor-
row morning when the baggage and cargo were un-
loaded, he, too, was going ashore, and he wasn't
coming back.

Nearby he could see the lights of Cincinnati,
but to the north all was darkness. That was the direc-
tion he must take.

His youth had been wasted in slavery, thought
William. When he looked back over his experiences, it
seemed to him he had already lived a lifetime, though

he was only about nineteen. He wasn't sure of his age, but he believed he had been born in 1814, in the autumn. Now fully grown, he was only of medium height, but strangers often turned to look at his face with its well-cut features and dark, piercing eyes.

After a last long look at the Ohio shore, William went below deck and counted over the small amount of money he had managed to save. Besides the money, he had a cloth bag into which he packed some dried beef, crackers, cheese, and a tinderbox. Then he tried to sleep, for he knew he would need his strength.

The sailors were at work early the next morning. The gangplank was lowered to the wharf, and the passengers and crew hurried ashore.

William picked up a trunk, and carrying it on his shoulder, strode onto the dock. When he was well away from the ship, he lowered the trunk to the ground.

For a moment he stood beside it, and then, when no one seemed to be watching, he walked away, trying to look as if he had been sent on an errand.

He turned onto the nearest street and headed north as he had planned the night before. Soon the houses thinned out, and the street ended. Directly ahead was a woodland. With a glance over his shoulder to make sure he wasn't being followed, he plunged into the shelter of the trees where he sat down to wait for darkness. Even though his skin was so light he could almost pass as white, he wouldn't risk traveling by day.

He had learned from experience that it was better to travel only at night. Last spring he and his mother had tried to escape to Canada. They had made a good start too, but 150 miles from St. Louis they decided it was now safe to travel by day. Almost at once they had been caught and returned to their masters.

William had been tracked down once and returned to his master. This time he planned his escape carefully.

William couldn't bear to think of his mother, for after their attempted escape, she had been sold far to the South. Slaves sent South to work in the cotton and sugar plantations didn't live long. Before she left, she had begged him to try to escape alone.

His sister Elizabeth, too, had been taken to the Deep South. Two of his brothers had died, and the remaining three were still slaves. He was sorry to leave his family behind, but there was nothing he could do for them.

As soon as it was dark, he started down a narrow path through the woods. When he reached a well-worn road, he headed north, following the North Star.

It was January, and he had no overcoat, but in spite of hunger and cold, for over a week he continued to walk toward Canada and freedom.

Within a few days his feet were frostbitten, his food was gone, and he had a bad cold. At last he knew he would die unless he had help.

Hiding behind some logs and brush near the road, he watched until he saw an old man he thought he could trust. Luck was with him, for the man was Wells Brown, a kindhearted Quaker who took the young fugitive home. He and his wife cared for William until he was well. They bought him new boots, and the wife made him some clothes.

Before William left, the Quaker asked, "What is thy name besides William?"

"I have no other," said William. "My father was a white man, a relative of my master. I'd rather be nameless than take his name."

"Thee must have another name. All free men have at least two names," said the Quaker. "I'll give thee mine and call thee William Wells Brown."

William left the Wells Brown home with new clothes, a package of food, some money, and improved health. But he treasured his new name above all his other gifts.

In a little over a week, he arrived at Cleveland, Ohio, on the shore of Lake Erie. On the far side of the frozen lake was Canada.

3. Secret Cargo

Lake Erie was covered with ice. William could see that no steamboat would travel on the lake for several months. His money was gone, and the weather was too stormy for him to walk to Buffalo, the nearest point for entry to Canada. Besides, he believed he was far enough north to be safe from recapture. So he decided to stay in Cleveland for the rest of the winter.

He was cold and hungry most of the time, but no discomfort could spoil his joy in being free.

William was forced to spend the winter in Cleveland.
Just across Lake Erie was Canada—and safety!

"I can get a job for myself," he thought, "and at last I can keep my wages."

On his first job he had no wages to keep. He worked as a general handyman for a family in exchange for his room and meals. At first this satisfied him, for it was a comfort to have a place to sleep and enough to eat after his long, cold trip North.

But he soon began to look for a better position. At a hotel, the Mansion House, he was offered a job as a waiter. He would receive only room and board at first, but if he did well, he might later be given a salary.

William accepted the challenge. He had waited on tables before, in Dr. Young's house and on steamboats on the Mississippi, so he knew how to please the people who ate at the Mansion House. He was quick and pleasant, and once in a while when the gentlemen talked to him, he made a witty remark that amused them.

In a short time his employer offered him a salary of twelve dollars a month.

When he received his first month's pay, William had a new feeling of freedom. He hid some of the money in his room, and with the rest in his pocket, he went to the newsstand and said proudly, "I'd like to buy a newspaper, please."

That night after his work was done, he went to his room and studied the newspaper. There were many words he couldn't read, but he worked at it by the light of a candle until his eyes blurred.

The next day he found a bookstore and bought a book. Whenever he had free time, he spent it reading.

One day one of the other workers at the Mansion House said, "Here's a newspaper for you. It's all about slaves and how to help them get free." He gave William an old copy of an antislavery newspaper called *Genius of Universal Emancipation*. It was published weekly by Benjamin Lundy.

A whole newspaper about the struggle against slavery! William had heard of such papers, but this was the first he had seen. He read it eagerly and thoroughly—the articles about antislavery meetings, the stories of escaped slaves, the reports of antislavery leaders. With every word his admiration grew for the Abolitionists who worked so hard to put an end to slavery. He was happy to realize that there were others like his friends, Mr. and Mrs. Wells Brown. He wanted to take part in the struggle too.

"There must be something I can do to help other slaves reach safety," he thought.

One day in the spring he walked to the waterfront. The ice that had locked the harbor all winter was gone, and the wharf was a busy place.

"I could take one of those ships to Canada," thought William, "but why should I? No one has bothered me here."

He realized that his light color was a protection. All along the Canadian border slave catchers lay in wait for anyone with dark skin. Many escaped slaves had made the hard journey to the border only to face the heartbreak of being captured and returned to their masters.

Of course, he, himself, wasn't entirely safe. Enoch Price, his former master, might try to find him.

An idea came into William's mind like an inspiration. He would get a job on a lake steamer! He would be safer on shipboard, and he could help other fugitive slaves get to Canada!

That summer he worked as a steward on a ship on Lake Erie. It wasn't much different from the jobs he had had on the Mississippi, but now he was free and in a good position to help others become free.

Sometimes he would follow a black man whom he saw hiding in an alley or behind boxes on the waterfront. Then he would offer him a boat ride to Buffalo or Detroit where it would be easy to cross to Canada.

Most members of the crew of the steamer were sympathetic and were glad to help William hide the secret human cargo. Sometimes he paid a fugitive's passage from his own money.

During one of his brief stays in Cleveland that summer of 1834, he met a young woman named Elizabeth Schooner. She was charming, and William was lonely. He quickly fell in love with her. They married before the summer was over.

At first all went well. He was impatient for each lake trip to end so he could get home to Betsey, as he called her. When winter came, he was glad, for then the lake boats were icebound.

Finding winter work in Cleveland wasn't easy,

though, and William began to think about moving east to Buffalo, New York, a much larger city than Cleveland. There was more winter work for blacks in Buffalo, and it also would be convenient for his lake job since it was at the eastern end of navigation on Lake Erie.

Best of all, Buffalo was within easy reach of Canada. This was important, for William knew that his old master might yet try to capture him.

At the end of the summer of 1836, William moved to Buffalo with his wife and their new baby daughter Clarissa.

Many escaping slaves came to Buffalo. Some settled down there, but others couldn't rest until they had gone the few more miles into Canada. The number of fugitives increased constantly as word of freedom in the North spread from one plantation to another, and workers on the Underground Railroad became more plentiful.

The Underground Railroad wasn't a railroad, and it wasn't underground. It was a country-wide network of people with heart and courage. They hid the escaping slaves in their homes and helped them reach the next friendly house or "station" on their northward route.

William took a winter job, and he gave most of his free time to helping the escaping slaves. He and

Elizabeth made their home a station on the Underground Railroad, and they often entertained men and women who came to town to speak about abolition.

In still another way William tried to help the blacks of Buffalo. He had noticed that many people, both black and white, drank more than was good for them. This was an especially serious problem for the blacks because at best they found it hard to get good jobs. For a black who drank, it was almost impossible.

Temperance groups for whites were already popular. Members of these societies agreed not to drink and tried to persuade others to follow their example.

The Browns offered their home as a station on the Underground Railroad to shelter escaping slaves.

Elijah Lovejoy, publisher of a newspaper in Alton, Illinois, lost his life during this antislavery riot.

When William organized a temperance society for the black community, it quickly grew to 500 members. The temperance work took a great deal of William's time, but his main interest was still the abolition of slavery.

It was dangerous to be an Abolitionist. In 1837 William heard of the death of Elijah Lovejoy, the kindly editor for whom he had worked in St. Louis. Mr. Lovejoy had written in his newspaper that slavery should be abolished. Three times his printing presses were destroyed by proslavery mobs. Lovejoy had been killed protecting his fourth press.

William was shocked at the news. He reacted by working harder than ever for the cause for which Lovejoy had died. He believed he could fight more effectively against slavery if he were educated, so in every free minute he studied English grammar, mathematics, literature, and history.

After six years his speech and writing had improved so much that in 1843 he was offered a job as a lecturing agent for the Western New York Anti-Slavery Society. William accepted eagerly.

4. Hecklers and Rotten Eggs

One winter evening in 1844, William Wells Brown went early to the church in Aurora, New York, where he was to give a talk against slavery. He was thirty years old and had been lecturing only a few months.

When he opened the church door, he saw that the pews were already full. At first he was pleased to find so large an audience, but when he reached the platform and looked down at the people below, he saw that he was faced with a roomful of hate.

Nervously he listened to the introduction about him.

"William Wells Brown only ten years ago was a slave," said the chairman of the meeting. "Now he's doing his part to help other slaves by lecturing for the Western New York Anti-Slavery Society. He devotes his entire time to this good cause. I present to you, Mr. Brown."

Before William could say a word, the people in the audience began to cough, stamp their feet, and whistle.

An egg, too old to eat, broke with a "splat!" in his face. Yolk and white ran down his chin and onto his clean shirt. William took out his handkerchief and wiped it off.

A howl of laughter came from his tormentors.

Half an hour passed, and the noise continued. William felt his patience ebbing.

"You have to learn to handle a tough audience," the president of the Anti-Slavery Society had told him. "If you don't, you won't be any use as a speaker."

William wanted to be a successful lecturer. This was the best way he knew to strike a blow against slavery. It was also a way of making a living, for he received a part of the collections that were taken after his lectures.

Suddenly he had had enough. He leaped down from the platform.

"I wouldn't speak to you if you begged me!" he shouted. "If you were slaves, you'd never escape! You wouldn't have the courage. You're cowards! You're afraid to listen!"

Surprise made people catch their breath. William's voice cut through the silence, compelling their attention.

"When you were children, did you hear your mother's cries as she was whipped by a heartless overseer? I did! Were you ever hunted by bloodhounds? Have you been locked in a smokehouse until you couldn't see or breathe? I was, by a master who called that kind of torture 'Virginia Play'!"

William dropped his voice to its usual quiet level, but he went on speaking for an hour and a half while the audience listened to the story of his years in slavery and his escape. When he finished, the audience that had booed now applauded.

When he started toward the door, a man blocked his way. "Some of us were going to play a little trick on you when you left, Mr. Brown," he said quietly.

William raised his eyebrows inquiringly.

"Listen." The man stepped closer. "There's a fellow in the belfry with a bag of flour. When you reached the front door, I was supposed to give the signal and he'd drop it on your head."

"What signal?"

"I was supposed to say, 'Let it slide!'"

William Wells Brown—an
escaped slave who became
a lecturer and writer

"Let it slide," repeated William absently. "Why
are you telling me this?"

The man shuffled nervously. "Because now that
I've heard you, I know you've had enough trouble. And
I think you're a brave man." He backed away. "Good
luck, Mr. Brown."

William thanked the man and continued toward
the front door. Just ahead of him were several of the
town's leading citizens. Talking together, they reached
the doorway.

In a clear voice that carried well, William said,
"Let it slide!"

As if by magic a torrent of white fell through the air. It coated the heads and shoulders of the men and set them coughing and rushing into the open air.

One of the men, more quick-witted than the rest, didn't go outside. Instead, he ran up the steps to the belfry to find the guilty person.

In the excitement, William Wells Brown left the church and went down the street chuckling to himself. He was sure the next speaker would receive a more courteous welcome.

5. A Ride by Freight

The train conductor stopped at William's seat. "You can't ride in the coach," he said. "It's for whites only. You'll have to get off the train or go to the freight car."

William was on a lecture tour of Ohio and was due to give a speech in the town of Republic that day. The train on which he was riding was the only way to get there on time.

Picking up his suitcase and the book he was reading, William walked down the aisle with dignity and made his way to the freight car.

Finding a seat on a flour barrel, he opened up his book and continued where he had left off in Alexander Pope's *Essay on Man*. Every place he went, he carried a book. He read constantly to make up for the years he had lost as an uneducated slave.

The train was approaching Republic when the conductor came into the swaying freight car to collect William's fare. "That will be one dollar and twenty-five cents," he said.

William looked up from his book. "That's the coach fare. What's the charge for 100 pounds of freight?"

With a look of surprise the trainman answered, "Twenty-five cents."

William reached into his pocket. "I weigh 150 pounds, and I'm riding in the freight car, so I owe you exactly 37½ cents." He counted the change into the outstretched hand.

For a moment the conductor hesitated. He looked from the coins in his hand to William Wells Brown who had calmly returned to his reading. With a grunt, the trainman closed his hand over the money and stomped out of the car.

William was away from home for over a month on his lecture tour. Then he soon left Buffalo again for talks in western New York towns. He missed being with his wife and two daughters, Clarissa and Josephine.

His wife was lonely too, perhaps lonelier than he knew. In May 1847 William was attending a meeting of the American Anti-Slavery Society in New York City when he received a letter from her.

After reading it, he packed his bags at once and took the next train home. As he rode along, he reread Betsey's letter. Yes, it was true. She said she was going away, and unless he came home for the two girls, she would leave them with neighbors.

William felt sick with unhappiness, for the letter made it clear there was no hope for his marriage. Apparently she had found someone else. Perhaps Betsey would have been more contented if he hadn't left her alone so much, he thought. But what could he do? Lecturing against slavery was his work and his duty.

The Massachusetts Anti-Slavery Society had asked him to work for them, so now he decided to accept their offer. He moved to Boston and enrolled Clarissa and Josephine in an integrated school in a nearby town.

William was becoming well known among the people who worked against slavery. He became friendly with such leaders as William Lloyd Garrison, the famous white Abolitionist, and Frederick Douglass, an escaped slave who lectured and wrote against slavery.

For years William had read Garrison's newspaper, *The Liberator*, and he agreed with most of Garrison's ideas. Both men wanted an end to slavery at once, but neither believed in using violence or politics. They thought that by talking and writing against slavery, they could change public opinion. This would lead, they hoped, to freeing the slaves.

William was contantly improving as a lecturer. He spoke clearly, and his manner was calm but persuasive. Newspapers often praised his talks. After one of his speeches, delivered in June 1847, when he was about thirty-three, an article in *The Liberator* included these remarks:

> W. W. Brown spoke with his usual power and effect. . . . There is an expression of fine and true humanity in the face of friend Brown, that is most pleasant to behold, and which will commend him to the love of all good men, wherever he may go.

In his lectures William usually told the story of his life as a slave. People always seemed to find his experiences interesting.

He was sure his speeches were helping the antislavery cause, but he wished he could reach more people.

Another escaped slave, Frederick Douglass, had

William Wells Brown counted as his friends William Lloyd Garrison (top), the well-known Abolitionist, and also Frederick Douglass (bottom), an escaped slave who spoke out against slavery.

written his autobiography. Thousands of people were buying and reading it.

This gave William an idea. He, too, had a story he could tell of his sufferings as a slave. Writing it might be the strongest blow he could strike against slavery.

In June 1847 William finished the story of his life and gave it to Edmund Quincy for criticism. Quincy was well educated; he was an author and a well-known Abolitionist. He wrote to a friend concerning Brown's autobiography, saying it was "a terrible picture of slavery, told with great simplicity." There was, he said, "no attempt at fine writing, but only a minute account of scenes and things he saw and suffered, told with a good deal of skill and great propriety and delicacy."

Narrative of William W. Brown, a Fugitive Slave was published in 1847 by the Boston Anti-Slavery Office. William dedicated it to Wells Brown, the Quaker who had helped him during his flight North and had given him his name.

At once the book sold well. It was written plainly and directly, as William spoke. His writing style wasn't polished, but he knew how to tell a story. People who started his book became so interested that they couldn't lay it down.

One of the most interested readers of the

Narrative was William's master, Enoch Price. After reading it, he wrote a letter to one of William's anti-slavery friends, offering to sell William Wells Brown for $325.

Some people in Boston who knew William volunteered to pay for him so he would be safe from capture, but he refused indignantly.

"God made me as free as he did Enoch Price," William said, "and Mr. Price shall never receive a dollar from me or my friends with my consent."

6. The Fugitive Slave Abroad

The Universal Peace Congress opened in Paris, France, on August 22, 1849, with the famous French writer, Victor Hugo, as president. Eight hundred important men and women from all over the world gathered to discuss plans for putting an end to war for all time.

One of the delegates from the United States was William Wells Brown.

As William sat in the audience and listened to the speakers, he wondered what his master, Enoch Price, would think if he knew his slave was an honored member of this congress.

It was partly because of his master that William was in Europe. His friends in the Anti-Slavery Society had been worried that Price might have William kidnapped and taken back down South. They had urged him to go to England to lecture against slavery, and finally he had agreed.

Many Abolitionists and former slaves went on speaking tours of England to raise money to carry on the fight against slavery in the United States. They were warmly received, for slavery had been abolished in all British possessions in 1833. Most Englishmen wanted to see the end of slavery in the United States. British sympathizers sent money to help American anti-slavery societies and paid for the support of fugitive slaves who came to England.

William Wells Brown knew he would have no trouble getting speaking engagements, for William Lloyd Garrison and other well-known Abolitionists had written letters of introduction for William to give to important people in England.

William agreed it would be sensible for him to get out of the country for a while. So when he was invited to attend the Peace Congress, he decided to combine the two activities.

All during the three days of the Peace Congress, the former slave received special attention. After the first session, Victor Hugo even came down from the platform to talk with him.

William went to England after the Peace Congress. There, many of the English delegates he had met at the congress entertained him in their homes and arranged lecture dates for him.

An English publisher printed copies of his book, *Narrative of William W. Brown.* The sale of his books and fees for his speeches would cover his expenses in London. Many fugitive slaves in England were supported by Abolitionist organizations, but William had too much self-respect to accept charity.

Usually he managed very well, but on at least one occasion he ran into trouble.

One Friday William sent ten pounds, about fifty dollars, to his daughters who were in school in Massachusetts. On Saturday he paid his rent. When he counted out his remaining money, he found that he had only a little change left.

He could manage for a few days, he thought, for on Tuesday evening he was to speak at a meeting in Worcester. He would be paid for his talk, and he would sell some of his books.

He went cheerily to find out about a train to Worcester which he had been told was only ten miles from London. At the station he received a shock.

"Worcester is more than 100 miles from here!" he was told.

William stared at the stationmaster. Then politely thanking him, he walked away. He didn't have nearly enough to pay his fare.

When he awakened Monday morning, he saw thick fog pressing against his windows, but no matter how bad the weather was, he had to go out. He must find someone who would lend him enough money to pay his way to Worcester.

All morning he walked from one place to another, but instead of finding anyone from whom he could borrow money, he met a poor fugitive slave who had absolutely nothing. It was lunch time, and the man was hungry.

"Come on," said William. "I have just enough to buy two bowls of soup. Let's eat."

It was late in the afternoon when William groped his way through the fog to his rooms. He would have to give up his plans for going to Worcester. Worst of all, it was too late to get word to the people who had arranged the meeting at which he was to speak.

The hours of walking in the fog had made him hungry, but he had no money for dinner. It was lucky, he thought, that the landlord supplied tea and biscuits to his tenants.

After tea, William, still hungry, had just settled

down with a book, when a visitor arrived. He was the son of the minister of a church where William had spoken not long before. After the lecture the young man, all on his own, had sold a number of copies of *Narrative of William W. Brown.* He had come to bring William the money from the sale of the books.

After thanking him, William said, "Come out to dinner with me."

"Thank you," replied the young man. "I've just had dinner."

As soon as his visitor left, William flung on his coat and dashed out for a hearty meal.

According to the October 26, 1849 *Liberator,* William's talk in Worcester was a great success. The article said that William "addressed the meeting for upwards of an hour and a half, being listened to during the whole time with the utmost interest, and on resuming his seat was loudly cheered."

William was still in England in 1850 when the Fugitive Slave Law was passed. His friends in America wrote to say, "Don't come home!" He would be in even more danger than before, they told him. This law forced the people of the North to return runaway slaves or be subject to a heavy fine or imprisonment or both.

So William stayed in England. In 1851 his

daughters came to England, too, to go to school. He continued to work hard to earn a living and pay for their education. Besides giving more than 1,000 lectures during his years in England, he wrote about America for London newspapers. Since he wasn't an experienced journalist, he often had to work all night to get his articles into shape to suit the editors.

In 1852 he spent a few months traveling and lecturing in France, Germany, and Italy. That same year his book, *Three Years in Europe; or Places I Have Seen and People I Have Met*, was published in England and Scotland.

This book was a collection of letters he had written to newspapers and personal friends telling about his experiences abroad. Sometimes his descriptions of famous people he had met were biting. He was especially critical of the writer Thomas Carlyle because he disliked Carlyle's attitude toward slavery.

Three Years in Europe sold well in England, partly because of the interest in slaves aroused by *Uncle Tom's Cabin*. People wanted to see what kind of book a former slave had written.

Some critics liked the book; others did not. The *London Daily News* said he wrote "with ease and ability." However, another English critic declared that William Wells Brown "pronounces judgments on men and things of which he knows very little with the forwardness of a schoolboy."

In November 1853 William published his first novel, *Clotel, or the President's Daughter: A Narrative of Slave Life in the United States.* The story was based on the rumor that President Thomas Jefferson had been the father of a girl who was born to a slave. To this story William added events from his childhood, stories from the lives of other slaves, and fiction. His purpose,

The title page of Brown's first novel, *Clotel*

CLOTEL;

OR,

THE PRESIDENT'S DAUGHTER:

A Narrative of Slave Life

IN

THE UNITED STATES.

BY

WILLIAM WELLS BROWN,

A FUGITIVE SLAVE, AUTHOR OF "THREE YEARS IN EUROPE."

With a Sketch of the Author's Life.

"WE hold these truths to be self-evident: that all men are created equal; that they are endowed by their Creator with certain inalienable rights, and that among these are LIFE, LIBERTY, and the PURSUIT OF HAPPINESS." — *Declaration of American Independence.*

LONDON:

PARTRIDGE & OAKEY, PATERNOSTER ROW;

AND 70, EDGWARE ROAD.

1853.

as always, was to arouse people against the institution of slavery.

The book was not a great success in England. Critics complained that *Clotel* contained too much material for one book, though they had to admit that it was interesting.

In the meantime, the news from home made William feel that he was standing on the sidelines while others fought for freedom. Yet, if he returned to the United States, he might be forced into slavery himself. At last he decided he must give his consent to some of his English friends who wanted to buy his freedom from Enoch Price.

In the summer of 1854 he received his free papers, and in September he boarded a ship for the United States. He was alone, for his daughter Clarissa was teaching school in England, and Josephine was studying in France. His estranged wife had died in 1851.

As he watched the Liverpool docks disappearing in the distance, he thought how happy he had been in England where he had been "recognized as a man and an equal."

He would miss his English friends, but he was ready to take up again the struggle against slavery in the United States.

7. "Show Your Colors"

The play was called *The Escape; or, A Leap for Freedom.* It told the story of the problems of three slaves and their flight to Canada.

William Wells Brown, the author of the play, presented *The Escape* as a dramatic reading before audiences all over New England. He took all the parts from heroine to villain.

This drama was just one more attempt by William to arouse people against slavery. When he used it as a dramatic lecture, his acting ability, his splendid voice and likable personality made people overlook the weaknesses of the play. But when *The Escape* was put into print, readers found that the language was stiff and unnatural, and the story was preachy.

Now that William was in the United States and a free man, he was giving more talks than ever before. He lived in Cambridgeport, Massachusetts, but he traveled from place to place so much he scarcely needed a home.

The Abolitionist societies were more active than ever, and William's stay abroad had increased his popularity. People who knew him remarked that he had improved in appearance, conversation, and speaking ability during his five years abroad.

His daughter Josephine came to visit her father for a while and sometimes spoke from the platform with him. While in America, she completed a book she had started in France, *Biography of an American Bondman, by His Daughter*. This book was soon published in Boston. William was fond of his two girls, and he was especially proud of Josephine.

Another young woman had recently come into his life. She was Annie Gray, also of Cambridgeport, and in 1860 she and William were married. She was twenty-five, about twenty years younger than William. Soon after their marriage they moved into a house in Cambridgeport next door to Annie's parents.

When the Civil War started in 1861, many blacks wanted to volunteer at once to fight for the Union. William urged them to wait, as he said the government hadn't yet proved it would bring about the freedom of the slaves.

On January 1, 1863, President Abraham Lincoln issued the Emancipation Proclamation which abolished slavery. After this William helped recruit black soldiers for the Union army.

Now William could foresee freedom for the slaves, and he began to think of their future as free men. He believed that they would need to build up pride in themselves and their background. He thought

"The Emancipation Proclamation." The famous document encouraged William to continue his fight for justice.

that white people, too, should learn more about the accomplishments of blacks so they would realize that a person's ability had nothing to do with the color of his skin.

With this in mind, he wrote *The Black Man: His Antecedents, His Genius, and His Achievements.* This book contained a short biography of William Wells Brown, plus sketches of the lives of fifty-three other blacks. Most of them were American or Haitian, and they ranged from Benjamin Banneker, the Maryland mathematician and astronomer who helped survey the site of Washington, D.C., to Phillis Wheatley, the poet, and Touissant L'Ouverture, the Haitian patriot.

Readers complained that *The Black Man* had errors and that Brown had left out some of the most worthy blacks. It was, however, a book that was needed at that time, and it sold well.

William himself was living proof of black intelligence and energy. For now in his fifties, he began to study and practice medicine.

He had been interested in medicine ever since he had helped his master Dr. Young care for the other slaves. Now he studied with other doctors and began to care for his friends and neighbors. A license to practice medicine was not required in those days.

In 1865 the Civil War ended, but people soon realized that it had not brought an end to all of the problems connected with slavery. William Wells Brown was one of the first to see the situation clearly.

On a cold January day in 1867, William dressed in his best clothes. The Massachusetts Anti-Slavery Society was holding its annual meeting that day, and he was going to give a speech. The meeting was to be in Boston, not far from Cambridgeport where William and his wife Annie lived.

As he buttoned his shirt and put a neat part in

his dark, curly hair, he thought about what he would say.

Unconsciously he spoke aloud. "Negroes took up arms because they were promised freedom, but blacks in the South are worse off than before the war!"

Annie came to the bedroom door. "I wouldn't think you'd need to practice," she said with a smile. "After all the speeches you've made, you can lecture in your sleep."

William put his arm around her waist. "You're right, Annie. But this is a new crisis. Conditions in the South are terrible. I don't blame Congress. I lay the blame right at the door of President Johnson. The only hope for blacks is to get the vote. Then we can elect a president who'll help us."

Annie sighed. "You do your part, that's sure."

She looked wistful, and William knew she was thinking of the days she had to spend without him when he was lecturing. Although his topics were different now—heroic black men in history and the need for blacks to have the right to vote—he was almost as busy giving speeches as ever. He was grateful that Annie believed in the importance of his work.

He was writing as well as speaking. Some of his books grew out of his talks. *The Negro in the American Rebellion: His Heroism and His Fidelity* was one such book. Later he wrote *The Rising Son; or, The Antecedents and Advancement of the Colored Race*, a history of black Africans.

Together, the two books contained short biographies of 110 blacks whose names and work might otherwise have been lost to history. Unfortunately, William's research was not thorough, and there were many errors. The books were useful mainly for the human interest stories they contained.

William rewrote *Clotel* too. The fourth version, which he called *Clotelle; or The Colored Heroine*, was dedicated to Annie.

In 1879, when he was sixty-five years old, William set out on a trip to the South. He was going to give talks on temperance, for since the end of the Civil War, he had renewed his interest in this cause. Also, he wanted to see for himself how conditions were in the South.

When he came home, he wrote a book about his trip—*My Southern Home: or The South and Its People.* He included stories of slave days and Negro folk songs, but he also gave his impression of conditions in the South. He declared that the southern states were taking away the political and social rights of the blacks. The races should work together for the good of all, he said.

He urged the blacks, who had been held down so many years by slavery, to pull themselves up by education. They should read good books, he told them, and stay away from drink. Most of all they should be proud.

He advised, "Black men, don't be ashamed to show your colors, and to own them."

My Southern Home was William Wells Brown's last book. But he continued to lecture on temperance and civil rights until a few months before his death at seventy years of age in November 1884.

For years the books of William Wells Brown were almost forgotten. His main topic was slavery, and when the slaves were set free, people lost interest in reading about the subject.

In recent years, however, a new interest in black history has arisen, and Brown's books are again being read.

Many black writers who came after him wrote better, but William Wells Brown is important as a pioneer—the first American black novelist, playwright, travel writer, and historian.

Charles Waddell Chesnutt
WRITER WHO CHOSE TO BE BLACK

1. I'm a Writer!

"I looked at your story," said the editor. "In fact, I got interested and read it all the way through." He gathered up the handwritten manuscript that lay on his desk. "It isn't bad for a young fellow."

Fourteen-year-old Charles Chesnutt asked hopefully, "Then will you print it in the paper?" His face was hot with excitement, and the palms of his hands felt damp.

The editor pushed up his green eyeshade for a better look at the alert young writer. "I'll print it, but I can't afford to pay you."

Charles nodded seriously. "I don't mind. I just want it to be in the newspaper." He wasn't surprised that the editor couldn't pay him. It was 1872. The Civil War had brought an end to slavery, but most blacks were finding it difficult to make a living.

He left the office and walked down the street, glowing with happiness. The editor liked his story! Of course, the newspaper was only a small weekly published for the blacks of the town of Fayetteville, North Carolina. But most of his friends read it, and they would see his story. This was a beginning. That was the important thing. Charles was ambitious. He was determined to do something worthwhile with his life.

Almost unconsciously he headed for the bookstore. He had to share his joy with someone, and his white friend, Mr. George Haigh, owner of the store, would understand how he felt.

Charles had discovered the bookstore soon after the Chesnutts had moved to Fayetteville. They had come there from Cleveland, Ohio, where Charles had been born and where they had lived until he was seven. Now whenever he had had a few pennies of his own, he hurried to Mr. Haigh's store to buy secondhand books, for there was no library in Fayetteville. Mr. Haigh liked the intelligent, courteous boy and let him browse about the store whenever he wished.

Today the bookstore proprietor smiled delightedly when Charles told him about his story.

"Wonderful!" he exclaimed. "I know you're going to leave your mark in the world, especially if you get an education."

Seven-year-old Charles Chesnutt (left) and his brother Lewis posed together in Cleveland in 1865.

"I'll do the best I can," said Charles, and it was a promise. He knew how hard it was for even a light-skinned black like himself to get ahead. Education was his best chance.

He was now a student in the all-black Howard School which had been established after the Civil War by the Freedmen's Bureau. The school was named after General O. O. Howard, the commissioner in charge of the bureau. Later General Howard started Howard University in Washington, D.C., for black college students.

Money was scarce in the Chesnutt home, but so far Charles had managed to stay in school. His father believed in education, and the principal, Robert Harris, a light-skinned black like the Chesnutts, took a special interest in Charles. Mr. Harris had hired him as a part-time teacher to help with the younger children. When he wasn't busy as an assistant teacher, Charles studied with his own class.

This wasn't an unusual arrangement in those days, for trained teachers were scarce. Almost anyone who had a few years of education was allowed to teach school.

"My mother always said I should stay in school," Charles told Mr. Haigh. Then he stopped abruptly and turned away. Although she had died a year before, he couldn't think of his mother without an ache in his throat. If she were alive, how pleased she would be about his story! Education had been important to her. Charles remembered hearing the stories of her girlhood when she had secretly taught slave children to read and write, even though education for slaves was forbidden.

Charles glanced at the bookstore clock. He saw that it was time to leave if he wanted to walk the two miles to the Chesnutt farm in time for supper.

Most black farmers in those days were tenants, but Charles' father, Andrew Chesnutt, owned his farm and log cabin. The cabin was small, but it was home for Charles, his father and stepmother, and five brothers and sisters.

That night Charles waited until everyone was at the supper table. Then, trying to keep his face straight, he said, "I wish to make an announcement. You may not know it, but a famous author is sitting in this very room!" At this point he had to laugh at himself and tell them about his story.

For a few minutes no one paid any attention to the bean soup that was cooling in the bowls.

"Everyone at school will read it!" cried Lewis, who was only a year and a half younger than Charles.

His little brother Andy said in an awed tone, "Your name will be in the paper."

"I'm proud of you, son," said Charles' father. He paused, then asked, "Will you get paid for it?"

Charles was downcast. "No. He said he couldn't afford to pay me."

His stepmother seemed to understand how he felt, for she said quickly, "The important thing is that the editor liked Charlie's story."

"That's right," agreed his father. "That's all we care."

But Charles wished he had been paid, even a little. The Chesnutts were better off than most, for

Andrew Chesnutt and his father before him had been free. Still, there never was enough money to cover the needs of the growing family.

Andrew Chesnutt had fought for the Union in the Civil War. When the war was over, Grandfather Chesnutt had set him up in business in a grocery store in Fayetteville. But Andrew had given credit to too many customers, and he had lost the store.

Now he was finding it difficult to make a living as a farmer, for the soil on his farm was poor. For that matter, farmers all over North Carolina were having a hard time. New industries were thriving, but farmers were getting low prices for their products.

Charles realized that he soon would have to find a way to help with the expenses. Being a writer—that was a dream, he knew. It would be years before he could write well enough to sell his stories. He would study hard at school, and after school hours he would take any kind of job to earn money. He'd never give up the idea of becoming a writer, though. It was a dream, but he'd make it come true someday.

2. Shall I Pass for White?

For another year Charles was able to stay in school. Then his stepmother had a baby. That meant another mouth to feed.

133

Charles was teaching school to help support his family when he was only fifteen.

Charles went to his principal, Robert Harris, to tell him that he had decided he must leave the school.

"We can't get along on what my father makes on the farm," Charles told him. "Somebody else has to go to work, and I guess it's up to me." He managed to smile, though he felt sick inside. "I'm the oldest, you know, and I've been lucky to be able to stay in school till I'm fifteen."

Mr. Harris had the look of a scholar, but he was interested in people as well as books. "I don't like to have you go," he said. "I see too many of my good pupils leave to take laboring jobs that only use their muscles and let their brains go to waste. We can't let that happen to you."

"I'll do any kind of work, but I'd like to get more education too."

Mr. Harris said thoughtfully, "You're a good teacher, and if you stay in school you can keep on studying. The trouble is that I can't pay you enough here. Would your father let you move out of town?"

Charles was surprised. "Why—I guess so. I can ask."

"My brother Cicero is a principal in Charlotte," explained Mr. Harris. "I know he needs a teacher, and he can pay better than I can. I'll find out if he could use you, and in the meantime you see if your father would let you go."

Soon all the arrangements were made, and a short time later Charles moved more than 100 miles away to Charlotte, North Carolina, a town of over 10,000 people. He lived with Cicero Harris and his wife in a home that was rich with books and magazines and ideas. Charles was happy. He worked hard and sent home most of his pay to his family.

When summer came, he couldn't afford to take a vacation, so he found a school for black students in the country where the term lasted only two months.

Having school in the summer wasn't very satisfactory, for many children worked in the fields. However, summer was the time when the dirt roads were passable and when teachers were more likely to be available for the low-paying country jobs.

On the day before school was to start, Charles caught a ride in a farmer's wagon and traveled over the dusty roads to his school district. He had to board with the parents of one of his pupils. When he was shown his room, he was pleased and grateful, for he knew what a sacrifice it was for this poor family to give him a room to himself. Beside the clean, narrow bed were a chair and a table where he could work.

The country school was a plain wooden building with one room for all the grades. Charles went early the first day and had the room neat and the books and slates ready when the first pupils arrived. He greeted them as they came in—little children just starting school for the first time and others as old as he, for Charles was only sixteen.

All day he taught one grade after another. He tried to keep the students busy and interested so they wouldn't get into mischief. He had made up his mind he would keep order without using physical punishment.

That night, after he had prepared his plans for

the next day's lessons, he felt lonely. If only he had some friend to talk with.

"Well," he thought, "I've been wishing I had time to write. Now's my chance."

He took out a clean notebook and wrote in it all that had happened that day. Keeping the diary became a habit during the quiet evenings of that summer of 1874, and he added new notes or a poem every few days. On August 14 he included a short story which he called, "Lost in a Swamp, an Adventure." It turned out quite well, he thought, but he decided it wasn't good enough to send to a magazine.

Although Charles wrote that summer, he also read and studied. He was determined to learn Latin, French, German, and Greek. It was a hard struggle, for his schooling had given him only a bare beginning in languages.

Even after he returned to Charlotte, he continued to study and to keep up his journal. He practiced writing his ideas in French and German and even in shorthand, for he had bought a book on shorthand and had begun to learn it.

He had read in newspapers and magazines that there weren't enough shorthand experts. If he could learn to write shorthand, he reasoned, he should be able to get a good job up North at more pay.

Charles longed to go North. His father and mother had liked it in Cleveland. In the North a black person had a better chance than in the South, he thought. For that matter, up North no one would know he was black unless he told them.

On July 31, 1875, he wrote in his journal:

> Twice today, or oftener, I have been taken for "white." . . . I believe I'll leave here and pass [for white] anyhow, for I am as white as any of them. One old fellow said today, "Look here, Tom. Here's a black as white as you are."

Life as a white man would be much easier, but would it be right for him to pretend?

He carried on an argument with himself.

"Why not say I'm white? I'm about seven-eighths white, anyway."

"Yes, but there's the part of you that's Negro. Are you willing to turn your back on your family and friends?"

"I can accomplish more in the world if people think I'm white."

"But if a black succeeds, it encourages all blacks. Why not show the whites what a Negro can do?"

"That's a winning point!" exclaimed Charles, putting an abrupt end to his silent argument.

Even while he played with the idea of passing for white, he knew he would never do it. He was proud of his Negro blood, and besides, he was too honest to take the easy way.

When he was nineteen, he was given an excellent job as assistant to the principal of the new State Colored Normal School in Fayetteville. This training school for teachers used the top floor of the Howard School. Charles' friend, Robert Harris, was the principal, and Charles enjoyed working with him and with the young black students who wanted to become teachers. At the same time he continued with his own education.

He was especially eager to learn to speak German and French correctly, and for that he needed a teacher. That presented a problem—there was no college nearby that would accept a black student. When he tried to find private tutors, he discovered that most of them were white, and they wouldn't take a black student, even if he did look white.

Again and again he was told, "If I teach you, my white pupils will quit."

Once in a while Charles had the help of a brave tutor, but most of the time he had to study alone.

He did manage to find a music teacher, and by practicing on the school piano and the organ at Robert Harris' home, he learned to play both instruments.

During the day, of course, he taught in the Normal School. He soon noticed an attractive young woman who taught downstairs in the Howard School. She had a smooth, high forehead, a skin slightly darker than his, and expressive eyes. Her name was Susan Perry.

One day he asked if he could walk home with her. This was a very special girl, he realized. He liked the look of honesty that gave strength to her young face, and he found himself telling her his plans and hopes.

With the straightforwardness that was part of her nature, she let him know that she liked him, too, and found him attractive.

This was the girl for him, Charles knew. On June 6, 1878, Charles Waddell Chesnutt and Susan Perry were married.

3. The Urge to Succeed

Charles no longer thought of passing for white, but he hadn't given up his hope of going North to live.

In the spring of 1879, he and Susan expected their first baby.

Charles Chesnutt was a pupil, a teacher, and then the principal of Howard School (below) in Fayetteville.

"I tell you, Susie," he told his wife. "Now we have to go North. Our child's going to grow up where there's a chance for equality."

"We'll find race prejudice up North too," Susan warned.

All the next year he worked on his shorthand. Hour after hour Susan read aloud to him so he could take down the words in shorthand.

As soon as school let out the next spring, Charles packed his suitcases and took the train for Washington, D.C., to look for work.

In the train he leaned his head against the back of the seat and thought about what he would do.

"I'll get a job as an official reporter for Congress. Or I'll work for some big newspaper. Then I'll send my brothers to college. And I'll build a fine house for Susie . . ."

A gust of wind blew through the open window beside him, bringing with it smoke from the engine. He waved his newspaper to clear the air, and when he could see again, he discovered his crisp white shirt-front was specked with cinders.

"This is very poor air for building air castles," he told himself wryly and settled down to read the paper.

In Washington he stayed with a friend who

lived in the middle of town. That first night Charles couldn't sleep because of the noise of carriages and horse-drawn drays in the street below his window.

The next day he began to look for work, but without success. His race wasn't the problem, for few people guessed he was a black.

"Let's see how fast your shorthand is," employers always said.

When Charles was tested, he was never fast enough. After two weeks, he realized he might as well go home. He was glad he hadn't given up his job at the Normal School.

Susan welcomed him joyfully, and Charles was happy to be home again with his wife and little Ethel. He eagerly told Susan about his trip.

"You must see the art gallery in Washington!" he told her. "And the museums!"

"I can wait," she said. "Right now I'd rather look at you."

He drew her closer. "Sometime I'm going to take you around the world," he promised her. "I'll work harder on my shorthand. Now I know how fast I have to be. When I can take down 200 words a minute, I can get a job anywhere."

"Charles!" Susan looked close to tears. "I was hoping you'd give that up!"

Charles shook his head. "I can't, Susie. It's my best chance to earn the kind of life we want. Look—do you want Ethel to have a good education?"

Susan nodded. "Of course I do! But we're happy here, and someday Ethel can go to the Normal School."

Charles got to his feet and paced up and down. "I'm not satisfied! We love music, and what chance do we have to hear it? I want to take you to see plays, and here everything like that is for whites only. There's no future for us in the South!"

That fall Robert Harris died. Charles Waddell Chesnutt, who was only twenty-two, became principal of the Normal School.

The next spring, on a day like many others, he worked at his desk at the school until late afternoon. Susan had dinner ready when he got home, but before he ate, he had to see the children. Ethel now had a sister Helen, who had been born in December.

He hurried through dinner, for he was reporting a lecture that night for the newspaper.

Susan tried to persuade him to stay home. He was always working, she protested, and it wasn't necessary. They had all the money they needed—and more.

That was true, Charles had to admit. His salary was seventy-five dollars a month, high pay for those days. Few black people were as well-off as he and Susan.

On the way to the lecture hall, he asked himself why he had such a restless urge to get ahead. The answer lay in his childhood, he guessed. He knew what it was to be poor, and he didn't want to be poor again.

Also, he seemed to hear his mother's voice saying, "Charlie, I know you can amount to something if you try. I hope you can help our people."

Although she had died when he was thirteen, already the pattern of his life had been set. He had loved his mother, and he wanted to carry out her wishes.

4. Two Hundred Words a Minute

Night after night Susan dictated to Charles so he could practice his shorthand. At last in May 1883, three years after his trip to Washington, he began to reach the speed he wanted.

For four nights in a row he took down 200 words a minute. Again on the fifth night he hit the 200 mark.

With a laugh Charles pulled Susan from her chair and gave her a hug.

"We did it, Susie! Now I'm ready to go North!"

She lifted a worried face to him. "You'll wait a while, won't you? Anyway, till after the baby comes in September?"

"I can't," he said gently. "The time to go is now, at the end of the school term. You'll be all right. You can stay with your father and mother till I have a good job and a place for us to live."

But it wasn't as easy to get away as he had expected. His father and his father-in-law both urged him to change his mind. And as soon as the news was out that Charles Chesnutt was leaving town, everyone tried to keep him in Fayetteville.

One man, whom he knew only slightly, stopped him on the street and said, "Mr. Chesnutt, you've been helping the blacks and whites in this town to understand one another. Please don't go now!"

His pupils at school didn't want him to go either. When he finally convinced them that his mind was made up, some of them surprised him by giving him an autograph album.

Trying to control his emotion, Charles held the little book in his hands and admired the cover with its decoration of birds and flowers. The watching students urged him to look inside, so he opened the album and read the first page:

Dearest Teacher:
    We, the following, present to you this album as a token of our love for you.

Charles felt his eyes burn. Many of the students were openly crying.

As he read on, he found verse after verse. Some were original, and some were not, but all were especially for him. In some, even the spelling was original!

One verse said:

Dearest Teacher,
These few lines to you are tendered,
By a friend cincere and true;
Hoping but to be remembered
When I'm far away from you.
     Your faithful scholar
     Emma Council

Another entry was not rhymed:

Dear Teacher,
  That your life may long and happy be and filled with success is the wish of your
     Sister and pupil,
     Mary Chesnutt

Was he doing the right thing? Charles wondered. He was needed here, and was wanted, more

The beautiful Chesnutt children—Ethel, Edwin, and Helen—soon after the move to Cleveland

than he had realized. But he knew, too, he would never be satisfied until he tried to make his way in the world outside. He wrote a letter resigning from his job as principal and then headed for New York City.

He found a room and went out at once to look for a job. He had letters of recommendation from friends in Fayetteville, but best of all he had his 200-word-a-minute speed in shorthand.

Before long he had a job in the office of Dow, Jones and Company, an agency that distributed news about Wall Street. It was located in the heart of the financial district of New York City.

Charles liked his work, and during his lunch hour he often found time to visit the New York Stock Exchange and to talk with other workers on Wall Street. People were always happy to make friends with this witty and kind young man.

One evening Charles wrote a short article about his conversations and experiences in the financial district and took it to a newspaper. The editors liked the article and asked him to write a daily column of Wall Street gossip for the New York *Mail and Express.* He would have preferred to write short stories, but at least he was writing and getting paid for it.

Often at night he took long walks on the still busy streets. He was lonely for Susan and the children. The new baby born in September was a boy, Edwin.

Where can we live? he wondered. The children of New York played in the streets and dodged the carriages. He wanted his children to have grass and fresh air.

"I can't bring them here," he decided. "Perhaps a smaller city would be better."

At once he thought of Cleveland. People there, both black and white, had been friendly to his parents.

In November he moved to Cleveland. Again his shorthand won him a good job, this time in the accounting department of the Nickel Plate Railroad.

Every night after work he hurried to his room to see if there was another letter from Susan. She wrote to him often, and every letter told how much she missed him.

In one letter she said:

I have found out since you left what you were to me. You were a companion, and you knew me better even than my father or mother, or at least you were more in sympathy with me than anybody else, and my failings were overlooked. No one can tell, my dearest husband, how I miss that companionship.

Once again Charles added up the small amount of money he had managed to save. It wasn't much, but it would have to do. He searched the city until he found a little house to rent. When he had furnished it with secondhand furniture, it still looked bare, so he bought bright material which he had made into curtains.

He had arranged to meet his family in Richmond, Virginia. Just before he left for the train, Charles walked nervously from room to room. The new window curtains looked fine, but the furniture was shabby, and there wasn't enough of it. He pictured Susan in that chair with the lumpy cushions and the children playing on the threadbare carpet. He made a vow to himself that soon he would have a better home for his family.

5. Lawyer and Writer

Every evening Charles played with his three children and read to them. When they were in bed, he studied his law books. He was now working in the legal department of the Nickel Plate Railroad and had begun to study law. He didn't have to go to school to do this, because a friendly lawyer had offered to help him and let him study in his office. Charles could study there until he was ready to take the examination.

One day he read in a Cleveland newspaper of a short story contest for new and unknown authors.

"Look here," he said to Susan. "I think I'll enter this contest. I'm new and unknown, that's sure." He was twenty-seven years old, and it seemed to him that if he was going to be a writer, he had better get some stories into print.

"Uncle Peter's House," the story which he sent to the contest, was one on which he had been working for some time. It told about the struggle of a black man, a former slave, to build a home of his own. At the end the hero, Uncle Peter, fell from a scaffold while working on the house and was fatally injured. Before he died, he asked his son to finish the building for his mother.

"Uncle Peter's House" didn't win the prize, but the people who ran the contest bought the story for ten dollars. It was printed in the *Cleveland News and Herald* and several other newspapers around the country.

At last Charles had a start. Now he wrote one story after another and sold most of them. The pay was small, but he was happy that editors liked his stories well enough to print them.

In spite of the time he spent writing, he was still working hard on his law studies. When he took the bar examination, he passed with the highest score of any of those who took the test that year.

On the night after Charles received word of passing the test, he and Susan had a long talk.

"I have to decide what I'm going to do next," he began. "I could set up a law practice, but I've been thinking about something else."

Susan said nothing, but kept on mending a sock. How patient she was, Charles thought.

It takes a patient woman to put up with all my ideas, he acknowledged to himself.

"I've been thinking about going to England to live," he went on. He watched her face for her reaction.

She didn't look as surprised as he had expected. "To get away from race prejudice?" she asked, glancing up from her sewing.

He nodded. "I hear there's very little feeling against blacks in England. I'm sure I could make a living, and it might be a better place for the children."

"But to leave our country—and our parents—" She dropped her sewing into her lap. "Oh, Charles, I don't know."

They talked for a long time, considering all sides of the question. At last he said, "Going to England— it would seem like running away, wouldn't it?" He got up and went to the window to stare out at the dark, quiet street. "Other Negroes can't go, so why should we? I think I'd be prouder of making a success here. And maybe we can do something to help the others, the ones who aren't as lucky as we are." He whirled around to face her. "Let's stay here."

"Good!" exclaimed Susan. She let out a sigh of relief and took up her sewing again.

Charles left his job at the Nickel Plate Railroad and rented an office. He began to build up a law practice and at the same time started in business as a legal

The library of the house in Cleveland where Charles wrote all his books

stenographer. His knowledge of law was a help when he went to court and took down the arguments of the lawyers, the testimony of the witnesses, and the words of the judges. His quick and accurate shorthand kept him in demand, and soon he had to hire other shorthand experts to help him. His stenography business grew faster than his law practice.

He was making such a good living that he was able to buy a new house, but money didn't take away his desire to write. He *had* to write, and he believed a black writer could do more to help his people than a black businessman. As busy as he was, Charles did not forget the people he had left behind in Fayetteville.

He and Susan kept in touch with their families, and now and then their parents came to visit. In 1888 Charles' sister Lillie moved to Cleveland to live with him and Susan. He took her into his office and taught her shorthand and typing.

Often Charles thought of the blacks he had known back in North Carolina. He remembered how the men had gathered around the stove in his father's grocery store. Most of them were poor and uneducated. Sometimes they talked about magic and told strange tales of witchcraft—"conjurin'" they called it.

One night Charles wrote a story based on one of the conjure tales he had heard. He called it "The Goophered Grapevine." In it one of the characters, old Uncle Julius, told how the grapevines were bewitched or "goophered" to keep the slaves from stealing the grapes.

The story was light and full of humor, but it was sad too, for it showed how hard life had been for the slaves. As he wrote, the black people he had known in North Carolina came to life on paper. The warmth of his feelings for them glowed in every word.

"The Goophered Grapevine" was accepted by

the *Atlantic Monthly,* one of the best literary maga-zines in the United States. It was the first time the magazine had printed fiction by a black American. The readers didn't know anything about the author, though. Charles made no secret of his race, but the editor thought it best to say nothing about it.

"I don't like passing as white on paper," Charles fumed. "But at least they're not whitewashing Uncle Julius."

Readers liked the story. It was different from anything they had ever read, and they sent letters praising it.

Charles wrote more "conjure" stories, and the *Atlantic Monthly* gladly bought them.

In 1891 he mailed a collection of eight of his short stories to a book publisher. He thought they might be made into a book.

But the stories came back to him with a letter. The editor advised him to keep on publishing in maga-zines until he was better known.

So Charles continued to write for magazines. One particular story had been growing in his mind for a long time. It was about a brother and sister, John and Rena Walden. Their mother was black and their father a white man. Both children were light-skinned. In the story John decided to ignore his Negro blood and became a lawyer, accepted by white people. Rena chose to remain in the black world. Charles understood these characters well, for like John and Rena, he, too, had had to make a choice.

This story became so long that Charles decided it had to be a novel. When he finally sent his manuscript to a publisher, they turned it down, but Charles wasn't discouraged. He continued to work on *Rena Walden* off and on during the next few years, for he felt he must make people understand what it was like to be neither black nor white, but a mixture of both.

Though he wrote almost every night and sold many of his stories, Charles found that he wasn't making much money with his writing. He now had four children, and he wanted them to have a good education. As the time for college drew near, he was especially glad he had his law practice and his legal stenography business.

When his two oldest children, Ethel and Helen, began their senior year in high school, Charles said, "How would you like to go to Western Reserve University?" As this school was in Cleveland, they could continue to live at home. "I expect many of your high school friends will go there," he remarked.

Ethel and Helen looked at each other. Finally Ethel said, "No, thanks. We've talked it over already, and we'd rather go to Normal School. That doesn't take four years, so we can start teaching sooner."

"Yes," agreed Helen. "Why drag through four more years of school if we don't have to?"

"*Drag* through!" exploded Charles. "I thought you loved school! You've always done well." His dark, piercing eyes demanded the truth. "You don't have to pretend with your mother and me. Why don't you want to go to Western Reserve?"

Helen said hesitantly, "We don't want to hurt you, but some of our white friends don't think we're as good as they are."

"Oho!" said Charles. "So that's it!" He felt a sharp pang of remorse. He should have taken his family to England to live.

Their beautiful nine-room house was in a white neighborhood, and they were warmly accepted by their neighbors. The best clubs in Cleveland had invited Susan and him to join. But now this!

After days of talking and planning, Charles and Susan suggested that the girls go to Smith College in New England where Charles was sure they would be welcome. Ethel and Helen liked this idea and agreed happily. Charles settled down to work harder than ever to pay the extra cost for their room and board out of town.

Charles Waddell Chesnutt—teacher, lawyer, public speaker, and author

6. Literary Pioneer

"One of the best short stories of the year!"

"'The Wife of His Youth' will become an all-time classic!"

Charles tossed down the reviews and turned to Susan with a grin. "That can't be my story they're talking about!"

He was forty-one years old, and now at last he was becoming known as a writer. That year, 1899, three of his books were published.

The title page of *The Conjure Woman*

THE CONJURE
WOMAN

BY

CHARLES W. CHESNUTT

BOSTON AND NEW YORK
HOUGHTON MIFFLIN AND COMPANY
The Riverside Press, Cambridge

The first was *The Conjure Woman,* a collection of his short stories about witchcraft. These stories showed the tragedy of slave life as few had told it before.

In the next book, *The Wife of His Youth and Other Stories of the Color Line,* the stories were mainly about light-skinned black people and their special problems.

The third book was a biography of Frederick Douglass, a famous slave who escaped and became a leader in the struggle to end slavery.

"All at once the publishers love me," Charles told Susan. "Now's the time to see if I can make a living at this writing business."

Again Susan had faith in him. "Go ahead and try it," she encouraged him.

So Charles closed his law and stenography office and set up his literary office at home.

Now at last he could work all day on his writing. For a while everything went well. Reviewers praised his books, sometimes comparing his writing with Mark Twain's in style and humor. People flocked to the book-stores for the latest Charles Waddell Chesnutt book.

One reviewer made it known that the author was a black man. This seemed to make readers even more interested in his work.

As his fame grew, he was often asked to give talks about his writing and the problems of blacks in America. Now at last, he was in a position to be of real help to other blacks. He gave lectures and readings from his books at literary societies, civic organizations, and in schools and colleges in Cleveland and all over the country.

Charles had strong beliefs, and he wasn't afraid to express them. Blacks, he told his audiences, were no longer slaves, but in many southern states their voting rights were being taken away. They were separated from whites in jobs, in schools, on trains, and in eating places and hotels. There was constant discrimination in the North as well.

The black *must* have all his civil and political rights, he insisted. On this point he even argued in public and private with his friend, Dr. Booker T. Washington, the black educator and founder of the Tuskegee Institute in Alabama.

Dr. Washington wrote to Charles, saying it was more important for a black to be able to make a living and bank his money than to vote. He said a man had to earn his bread every day, but he might vote only once every year or two.

Charles answered that ". . . the importance of a thing is not to be measured by the number of times

Booker T. Washington, the famous black educator. He and Charles did not always agree on what goals were most important for blacks.

you do it. Birth. Death. Marriage. You argue the question as though the Negro must choose between voting and eating. He ought to do both, and can do both better together than alone."

As successful as his lectures were, Charles thought that his strongest weapon in the fight for equal rights for blacks was his fiction. So he was especially happy when a publisher finally accepted the book about John and Rena Walden on which he had worked so long. It was to be called *The House behind the Cedars*.

In October 1900 the novel was published. At once it aroused a great deal of interest. Charles was the only well-known black fiction writer, and he could be expected to write with authority on the subject of the light-skinned black people. However, many critics said *The House behind the Cedars* was not as well written as the author's short stories. Many also felt that he had weakened his story by including so much about the unfair treatment of blacks.

In spite of its faults, Charles Chesnutt's first novel told an appealing story about a problem on which little had been written. Fan mail poured into Charles' office at home. Readers wrote to tell him how much they liked the story of the Waldens, and publishers asked to bring out his next book.

"You need a private secretary," Susan told him as she helped him open the letters.

"Wait till they read my next book!" Charles said with a laugh. "That will start some arguments. And," he added soberly, "I hope it'll bring in some money. Writing certainly doesn't pay as well as business."

Charles' new book was to be about the race riots that had taken place in Wilmington, North Carolina, two years before, in 1898. In order to get firsthand information about the riots, he made a trip to Wilmington and talked with many people.

The result was a fast-moving story woven around events before and during the riots. His aim was to show that the blacks were not to blame for the riots and that they suffered most from them.

The book, *The Marrow of Tradition,* didn't have a large sale. A famous literary critic, William Dean Howells, said the writing was good, but that the book was "bitter."

The mood of the times was against serious fiction. Readers wanted to be entertained, not made to think.

The poor sale of his new book made Charles face a sad reality. He and his family could not live on his income as a writer. People weren't ready to read about the troubles of the blacks, but he was going to continue writing about them. He would have to go back to stenography by day and writing by night.

Although he preferred writing, he was happy in the business world. His legal stenography office soon became so busy that he had little time for writing. In the evening he often sacrificed precious writing hours to give lectures on rights for black people before civic clubs.

Still, in the midst of this busy schedule, he managed to write another book, *The Colonel's Dream,* which was published in September 1905. It was a

Charles Chesnutt in the library of the house on Lamont Avenue where he spent his last days

tragic story of the futile attempts of an idealistic white man to reform a southern town and help its black inhabitants. To Charles' disappointment, the book sold poorly. Like his other novels, it was criticized for containing too much "propaganda."

In December of that same year, Charles received an unusual invitation. A publisher was giving a big party in New York City in honor of the seventieth birthday of their most famous writer, Mark Twain. Only 150 of the most outstanding writers in the United States were invited, and Charles was one of them.

What a party it was! The food was excellent. Mark Twain and the clever guests gave amusing speeches. Charles enjoyed most the chance to talk with the other writers. Many of them told him how much they admired his work, but that was no help in the sale of his books.

After the poor reception of *The Colonel's Dream*, Charles wrote less and less. He did write one more novel, but it was never published.

When he was fifty-two years old, Charles Chesnutt had a slight stroke and had to spend several weeks in the hospital. After that he wasn't as strong as before.

"You must take time to relax," the doctor said.

So Charles went to Europe. His daughter Helen went with him, for Susan found that long sightseeing trips tired her. She didn't want the trip around the world her husband had once promised her. She had always been happiest in her own home.

When he returned, Charles spent less time at his office, but he worked even harder than before for equal rights for blacks.

People in Cleveland, both black and white, appreciated his efforts. Although his writings and lectures had made him known all over the United States, his own city was especially proud of him.

Probably the greatest honor of his life came to him in 1928 when he was seventy years old. It was then that he received the Spingarn Medal, a national award.

Each year this gold medal is presented to "that Negro man or woman who by his or her individual achievement as judged by a committee, shall have reflected most credit upon the race in any field of honorable endeavor."

The medal was given to Charles Chesnutt because of "his pioneer work as a literary artist depicting the life and struggle of Americans of Negro descent and for his long and useful career as scholar, worker, and freeman of one of America's greatest cities."

Between the publication of *The Colonel's Dream* and his death at the age of seventy-four, Charles Chesnutt did little writing. His strong and lasting reputation as a writer had been built in the years 1899 through 1905 when the bulk of his work was published.

Although Chesnutt's career was short, it was brilliant. He is considered the most competent black writer of fiction before the 1920s. His work proved that writing ability had nothing to do with race or skin color. As a result, future black writers were taken more seriously and had a better chance of getting published.

As a man, Charles Waddell Chesnutt had the courage to stick to his convictions and the humor to do it gracefully.

He lived according to the belief he once expressed in a letter to Dr. Booker T. Washington:

> If the colored people ever expect to cut any figure in this world, they must not pitch their ideals too low; though their feet must of course rest on earth, it should not be forbidden to them to lift their eyes to the stars.

Index

DATE DUE

MAY 2 1 1990			